Bread & Water, Wine & Oil

AN ORTHODOX CHRISTIAN EXPERIENCE OF GOD

Archimandrite Meletios Webber

Conciliar Press ❧ Ben Lomond, California

Bread & Water, Wine & Oil:
An Orthodox Christian Experience of God
© 2007 Peter (Meletios) Webber

Published by   Conciliar Press
                   P.O. Box 76
                   Ben Lomond, California 95005-0076

Printed in the United States of America

ISBN 10: 1-888212-91-8
ISBN 13: 978-1-888212-91-4

Contents

Statement of Gratitude

ΤHE ONLY AUTHENTIC RESPONSE TO LIFE—THE GOOD bits and the not-so-good—is gratitude.

I owe immense amounts of gratitude to all those who have been my teachers, wittingly and unwittingly, throughout my life.

In particular, I want to thank the parish community of Prophet Elias in Santa Cruz, California, and most especially Christina Colyvas, Dr. Nicholas Itsines, and Prof. Rick Otte. I also offer heartfelt thanks to Fr. Jonah Paffhausen and the monks of the Monastery of St. John of San Francisco in Manton, California. I also want to pay tribute to the clergy and people of the St. Nicholas of Myra parish community in Amsterdam for their hospitality and great kindness.

Finally, thanks to all the people at Conciliar Press who have guided me through to the completion of this book.

In the book that follows, I have attempted to integrate some of what I have learned in more than thirty years as a priest of the Orthodox Church with what I have learned in my work as a psychotherapist.

Whatever is useful or helpful to readers of this little book I attribute to the wisdom of my many teachers. Whatever is not, I cheerfully accept as part of my own fallen, human condition.

ARCHIMANDRITE MELETIOS WEBBER

~: PART I :~

Life as Mystery ❧

~: CHAPTER I :~

The Mind, the Heart & Mystery

THE WORD "MYSTERY" CAN BE QUITE BAFFLING. LIKE ALL words, it is a pointer, but in this particular instance it is pointing at something that cannot be described, something that lies beyond the place where the mind can make sense of things.

Yet, this word "mystery"—together with its many levels of meaning and its profound significance—lies at the heart of the Eastern Orthodox experience of God. Those who come to Orthodoxy from another Christian tradition or from a Western educational background will do well to come to terms with this word before they proceed to make the most of the immense treasures of faith and practice Orthodoxy has to offer.

In everyday English, the word "mystery" implies a puzzle to be solved, a conundrum to be unraveled. The idea is that if you think about a problem long enough, you will find a solution. In the East, on the other hand, a mystery is an area where the human mind cannot go, where the heart alone makes sense—not by knowing, but by being. The Greek word *mysterion* leads you into a sense of "not-knowing" or "not-understanding" and leaves you there. Having arrived, all you can do is gaze and wonder; there is nothing to solve.

One of the most noticeable features of Eastern Christianity is that it is this word, "mystery," which describes those actions of God that have a specific, decisive, and eternal significance in the lives of those who take part in them. Everyday substances—oil, water, bread, wine—together with simple actions—offering, blessing, washing, anointing—are the means by which God intervenes in our lives. These interventions, in which God does all the work and our only contribution is to be prepared and present, color and shape our lives beyond the extent that would be possible in any human encounter. Moreover, unlike most human interactions, they do not take us from a place of ignorance to a place of knowledge. Rather, the Mysteries lead us deeper and deeper into the Mystery which is the presence of God Himself.

To speakers of English, it may seem oddly coincidental that the word "mystery" is used in the Orthodox Church to signify what most Christians in the West refer to as "sacraments." However, one of the most astounding transformations a human person can undergo happens when an enquirer realizes that the word "mystery" in all its dimensions is exactly what is experienced in Orthodoxy by the person who enters into and participates in the life of God in the life of the Church. The "Holy Mysteries" are precisely what they say they are.

When taking part in the Mysteries of the Church, Orthodox Christians do not experience mental exercise, nor are their emotions of any particular significance. Participation in the Mysteries is an encounter with God in a very intimate and direct way. As nearly as I can put it into words, such an encounter brings thinking and feeling to a halt, albeit briefly. As can happen when looking at something extremely beautiful, or when suddenly finding oneself in a life-or-death situation, thought and feeling are momentarily stilled, and something much more profound is engaged. The encounter penetrates through thinking and feeling and goes to the very being of the person taking part—to that fathomless state of awareness that exists, yet lies hidden and dormant, in all human beings. In Greek, this is what the Fathers called the *nous*. In this book, it will also be called the "heart."

Before we can begin to explore the Mysteries, therefore, we must come to a better understanding of the Orthodox conception of the nature and relationship of the mind and the nous or heart.

Like almost everyone alive, the great teachers of Orthodoxy saw that the world is not a perfect place. God is perfect in Himself, but His creation, the world about us, has some obvious flaws. The Fathers attributed this situation to the narrative in the first few pages of the Bible that tells the story of our first parents, "the man" and "the woman," Adam and Eve. Through a misuse of the freedom God had given them, Adam and Eve were expelled from paradise. We, their descendants, inherit and experience this state of exile with them until that moment when our participation in the life of Christ within the Church, and the healing that brings, leads us back to where we belong.

The way the Orthodox teachers look at the story of Adam and Eve is quite different from the way it is generally understood in the West. In the West, commentaries tend to emphasize the themes of disobedience, guilt, sin, and remorse, including a fairly heavy hint that the sin of our first parents was somehow sexual in nature—an attitude that would have enormous impact on the development of Western psychology many hundreds of years later.

For the East, by contrast, the story of Adam and Eve is, at its heart, a story of disintegration, fragmentation, and estrangement. The man and the woman—and the world in which they lived—were torn apart by their behavior, and vast gaps came to exist between God and man, between heaven and earth, between one person and another, between the genders, and finally even within the human personality itself. Each and every person is internally fragmented and externally isolated from the outside world, right down to the ultimate depths of his or her being. Fragmentation within the human personality is observed essentially as the division between the mind and the nous or heart.

∾: THE MIND AND THE NOUS :∾

In the broadest of terms, one might say that Western civilization is dominated by the human mind, and "knowing" generally takes precedence over "being." In the East, by contrast, experience is valued over thought. Rather than the mind, it is the nous of man—described by St. Makarios as the "eye of the heart" and identified by St. Diadochos as the "innermost aspect of the heart"—that is considered the most important element by which a person communicates with God. This crucial element, the center of spiritual intelligence, is all but ignored in Western writings. Western philosophers actually use the word *nous*, but when they do so it is little more than a synonym for "mind."

The nous—translated here as "heart"—is a theoretical body part with a very specific and special function. Its importance and its use, based on Orthodox patristic experience, lie at the heart of this book's theme.[1]

Western psychotherapy is often concerned not only with healing the mind, but also with encouraging patients to come to terms with their feelings and emotions. Moreover, at least in everyday speech, it is assumed that the source of these emotions or feelings is the heart.

In the East, we can discern another scheme. Here, the one thing that can be said of the mind is that it is divorced from the heart. In this fallen state, it issues a constant stream of *logismoi*, the torrent of "thoughts" that accompanies our daily lives. However, in a less demonstrable way (the Fathers do not really talk about emotions), the mind is also the source of emotion and feeling. These originate in the mind as logismoi which are then felt, in a reactive way, in the physical body; these reactions are what we call feelings. Feelings, then, in fallen man are as broken and unreliable as the thoughts that give them birth.

It is necessary to make a clear distinction between thoughts that we have when we make an effort to think; thoughts that have us, which seem to emerge automatically; and thoughts that come from an altogether deeper awareness which we may call discernment or intuition. Describing these three forms of thought (and there may be

---

1   The three essays of Bishop (now Metropolitan) Kallistos of Diokleia at the beginning of the book *Merton and Hesychasm; the Prayer of the Heart and the Eastern Church* in the Fons Vitae Thomas Merton series, 2003, precisely and accurately describe themes the reader may find unclear in the present book.

many others) is not simply a matter of theorizing about such things. The distinction between them has very important practical implications for our spiritual development.

Leaving the third to the experts (remembering that saints do not tend to advertise themselves), most people can recognize the difference between using thought and being used by thought. The ability to think logically plays an important part in our fundamental role as God's cocreators. However, the stream of automatic thoughts which almost all of us recognize in ourselves needs to be regarded with some suspicion, as, according to the experience of the Church, it originates from a mind that is broken, divorced from the heart. It is these thoughts (logismoi) of a person that eventually turn into passions—those behaviors that cut us off from God. They stand in opposition to passionlessness, which the Fathers envisage as a state on the path to spiritual healing. Passionlessness (in Greek *apatheia*) does not mean a lack of love or concern, as it tends to sound to Western ears, but rather a state of being unaffected by the passions as defined above.

The classical patristic expression of the relationship between thoughts and passions and the effect of one on the other is as follows: First of all, a thought comes to exist in the mind of a person, seeking that person's attention and awareness. There follows a period of *interaction*, during which the person dabbles in the possibilities the thought brings. The third stage is *consent*, where the person voluntarily gives in to the thought—sometimes hoping to stop the process immediately thereafter, only to discover that once embarked upon, this is very difficult. The fourth stage is *captivity*, in which the person is dragged further and further from the way of righteousness towards spiritual destruction as a result of the thought. The fifth stage, the goal of the thought, is labeled *passion*; here the person is entrapped, and sinful action is inevitable.

The ascetic authors often seem to talk about thoughts as if they arrived one at a time. However, we also experience undifferentiated streams of thought that follow the progression noted above, sometimes quickly, sometimes slowly, and often with many competing or even contradictory thoughts arising at any given moment. It is possible that this is a condition that has been experienced only in modern times.

Another symptom of modern living is the prevalence of addictive behavior in almost every area of human activity. The Fathers talk of the need to struggle with the passions, and indeed a powerful image of the spiritual life is that it is a constant struggle with the passions— the detritus of human thought. Here, however, it may be necessary to make a distinction between "passions" in the patristic sense and "addictions" in the modern sense. It is possible that addictions, as we now experience them, are of rather recent development and beyond the scope of the classical authors of ascetic literature. This factor is important, since the current knowledge about recovery from alcoholism, for example, depends on a process that might be termed "spiritual surrender," and not (as might be understood from reading the Fathers) on attempting to crush the addiction by willpower.[2] Struggling with an addiction only makes the addiction worse, as many have come to learn at the cost of their lives. This is a small but important point, since it may actually put people's lives in danger.

The patristic scheme of thoughts and passions outlined above, together with its progression, is logical and works well as a model for much of human behavior, whether we are looking at other persons, entire groups of people, or ourselves. However, it has little in common with methods employed in modern psychotherapy, for which sinful action is less important than feelings of guilt, low self-esteem, or depression, even if those conditions have come into being as a result of sinful action.

Where the two systems overlap, however, and provide us with a heightened awareness is in recognizing the following: The passions, moods, and emotional states that most often dominate the human personality have their origin in thought, that is to say, in the mind.

To the world at large, it would appear obvious that the mind is the dominant force in a human being, even to the point of identifying itself as the entire person. However, the teachers of Orthodoxy generally

---

2 For a further discussion of this topic, please see my book *Steps of Transformation* (Conciliar Press, 2003).

indicate that this is not the case, or at least not the whole case. As a result of the Fall, a definite and definable split has taken place between the body and the "person" (however that is experienced), and a vast abyss divides the heart and the mind. For the Orthodox writers, far from being the answer to all problems, the mind of man is the place where most of our trouble starts, and the path towards sanctity entails recovering the sense of intellect not in the head but in the heart. There, at the center of the life of the individual, is the point where he or she meets and communes with God. In its fallen state, the heart is weak and powerless, but nevertheless, it remains the most powerful spiritual element among all the parts of the human personality.

Through prayer and participation in the Mysteries of the Church, the human person receives the opportunity to start healing, and the grave division between head and heart diminishes. In God's time, the healing progresses to a point where the heart and the mind are reunited, and the original unfallen state of both is restored—now not merely in the original light of Eden, but in the transfigured light of the Kingdom of heaven. This is the Orthodox understanding of salvation.

❧ WHAT DOES FRAGMENTATION LOOK LIKE? ☙

In the field of mental health, there are a number of conditions that indicate the process of fragmentation in people in rather extreme ways. Schizophrenia, multiple personality disorder (now often called "dissociative identity disorder"), and borderline personality disorder are all examples of conditions in which individuals are obviously and seriously troubled by the fact that they are internally fragmented. More accurately, they are troubled not so much by their internal fragmentation *per se* as by the way they cope with it.

However, normal people also exhibit indications that fragmentation exists; it is not merely a problem for the mentally ill. Although generally fairly subtle, this phenomenon is most obvious when someone loses his or her temper, a condition that happens to almost all of us from time to time. On becoming very angry, people often feel a change occurring within themselves, and it is not uncommon for such a person to feel quite different, quite "other" than his or her normal self. Questioning such a person at that moment is often fruitless, since he or she is not "present" to be questioned; however, if the situation is discussed later, many will admit to having felt much younger, even like a child, during the time they were angry. The person who loses his or her temper actually experiences the world and events within it from a point of view quite different from the one he or she normally experiences. This may be because, at some time in the past, such people have learned that by entering a "child state" they are more likely to get what they want. Successful behaviors are the ones most likely to be employed again. At the very least, one may suppose that anger must have worked for them when they were children. Having learned a behavior that got them what they wanted, it is almost impossible to alter that behavior at a later stage, even when it has become entirely inappropriate and the grown-up is behaving like a child.

Let us have a look at another, perhaps less threatening, example. A woman speaking to her mother is not exactly the same person as when she speaks to her own child. Anyone who is present at a large family gathering will see individuals switching from being a child to being a parent with great ease. It is no huge psychological feat. I remember seeing a television program about the present queen of Great Britain that showed her attending a horseracing event. At one point she turned to her own mother, who had, one imagines, just made some sort of off-camera parental comment. She reacted just as any little child would ("oh Mummy!"), in a tone far removed from the regal dignity and bearing she more often exhibits. If this sort of behavior holds true for a queen, it probably holds true for the rest of us as well.

A third example of this process can be observed in people sitting in a church, a courtroom, or a doctor's waiting room. Most would agree that we are not quite the same people in those places that we are in the workplace, in a store, or in a restaurant. Actually, this phenomenon is most noticeable when someone does not go through the expected transformation in a place like that—a person who behaves in church just as he might in his favorite restaurant sticks out from the rest of those present, often causing great embarrassment to those around him.

In some respects, we might say that Western psychotherapy aims at healing the fragmentation of the mind. This it does by encouraging the acquisition of insight, and by the application of method, system, and sometimes even common sense to achieve a change in the person undergoing therapy.

Unlike conventional psychotherapy, however, the spiritual path of Orthodoxy does not stop at that point, since it is concerned not only with the workings of the mind but with the heart as well. Ultimately, healing from an Orthodox point of view must inevitably include the reunification (or, to borrow a term from computer technology, "defragmentation") of the human personality, including re-placing the mind in the heart (where it belongs). Indeed, this process is often described in the ascetic literature of the Orthodox Church as the ultimate purpose of prayerful effort (or "ascetic labor").

The process of fragmentation, which we inherited from our first parents, consists in thoughts being removed from the "mind-in-the-heart," where they belong, and placed in a state of semi-independence in the brain—where they reign apparently supreme, feeding (and in turn fed by) the ego. Through the practice of spiritual principles, the reversal of this situation is possible, but it cannot be brought about simply by an act of determination of our minds. Willpower alone is useless. I suppose it is axiomatic to say that we cannot use something that is broken to fix itself. Besides, any solution determined by our minds usually ends up as some sort of internal power-play and is doomed to failure. Healing is available, but it can only be powered by the grace of God.

∾ WHAT THE MIND DOES ∾

Since most modern people are accustomed to using their minds rather than their hearts to make sense of the world, it may be valuable to consider in greater detail how the mind works in practice.

The needs and desires of the mind are limitless. So are its fears. However, it needs to be said right at the beginning that the mind is not evil in itself. On the contrary, the mind is a beautiful and necessary part of human existence, and like everything else in the created universe, it was fashioned by God. The ability to use the mind is crucial in almost everything we do, even though we have not really begun to understand how it works. Obviously, the mind has an important connection with the brain, but in some senses the mind also seems to work throughout the body, affecting every cell, perhaps every atom of our existence, as it functions. Apart from anything else, the working of the mind underlines the immensely important relationship of co-operation between who we feel ourselves to be, as people, and our bodies. So long as we are alive, consciousness without the cooperation of our bodies seems to be, quite literally, unthinkable.

There are occasions, for example when we are driving, when it is obviously essential to have the ability to think, since we must constantly be making comparisons: measuring distances, judging how much gasoline to use, deciding when we need to apply the brakes in order to stop at a certain point, and so on. Analysis, from the most simple to the most complex, is achieved by the mind. At such times the mind is a like a very sophisticated computer, as good or bad as any other computer, depending on the skill of the user and the quality of the data it is dealing with.

However, it seemed obvious to our spiritual teachers, just as it seems obvious in the modern world, that there is something broken about the way the mind works, particularly in those situations where the mind seems to have a life of its own. Unlike a computer, the mind does not have an "off" switch. When we are not actually using it, it carries on under its own power, behaving as if it were in charge and issuing a constant stream of comments and challenges, almost all of which are of a negative character. As we have seen, the Fathers call this activity *logismoi*, and although these thoughts are not evil of themselves (most of them start as simple speculations of the "what if" variety), the spiritual experts maintain that all sin has its roots in this stream of thought.

The stream of thoughts is negative because the mind dwells in a land of unrelenting desire and boundless fear, and it attempts to influence us to experience these two areas as our rightful home. Almost anyone who has ever lain awake at four in the morning listening to the workings of the mind knows what this feels like. Some people actually hear an almost constant stream of conversation going on in their heads throughout the day, encouraging them to want and need, to be afraid, to feel alienated and alone. Many people experience the mind as a commentary. Still others, though denying that they can actually hear anything, will quickly agree that it is a very difficult thing to keep the mind quiet. Any attempt at counting from one to ten without having an intervening thought (including those inevitable ones like "gosh, I'm able to count without having a thought") will reveal just how difficult it is.

It is not until we learn to quiet our thoughts that there is even the possibility of learning to use our hearts. Apart from anything else, the mind uses noise constantly to reassure itself of its own existence. The language of the heart, on the other hand, is silence. Here I am not referring to an empty silence, one that is simply waiting for something to happen. Rather I refer to the overflowing silence, the silence that is the heart's means of communication, a full and profound experience of being, and a deep awareness of God.

∾ THE PRESENT MOMENT ∾

One noticeable way the mind works is that it rejects the here and now. This combines an undercurrent of negativity or dissatisfaction with a sense that the reality of God's world is not good enough. Indeed, the motto of the mind, if it had one, might very well be, "Anywhere but here; any moment but now." It lives in an environment of constant complaint and discomfort.

When the mind looks at the present moment, it sees nothing, or at least nothing worth considering. The present moment has no shape or form, so there is nothing to measure. Since defining things through labeling and measuring is the main task of the mind, when it comes to something formless, it simply ignores it. The mind prefers to work in the past or future, since these dimensions are both actually constructs of the mind's own workings and thus the mind controls them. The present moment, however, is completely outside its control and therefore ignored.

The mind is the guardian of memories and fantasies, the past and the future respectively. Memories and fantasies come in two (and only two) varieties: good and bad. This means that all desires (related to keeping good memories and creating good fantasies) and all fears (related to avoiding bad memories and bad fantasies) come within the jurisdiction of the mind.

Unfortunately for the mind, the present moment is the only moment that is, in any sense, real. Moreover, in spiritual terms, the present moment is the only possible occasion in which we can meet God (or anyone else).

The mind attempts to be almost completely absent from the present moment—this is actually what we experience when we lie awake early in the morning. All anxiety, all fear, all disturbance come from memory or from anticipation, from the past or from the future, but not from the present. The present rarely (perhaps never) poses a problem; it just presents a situation.

In our society it is not uncommon to meet people who carry huge burdens of pain around with them, all of which exists either in the past (as unhappy memories) or in the future (as anxiety). Society in general and their minds in particular do not announce to them that carrying this burden is actually an optional activity. We are not our thoughts. The pain such people feel is real enough, but actually exists only in their thought processes and absolutely nowhere else. It certainly does not exist in the present moment, the only part of their life that is "real" in all its dimensions. The present moment has many special qualities, but it is almost always full of joy. However, this joy, which is available to anyone and everyone, is for many people completely obliterated by the pain of the past or the future, urged on by the mind.

The movement of emotion further clouds the way the mind works as our bodies react to the thoughts the mind is producing. Whether felt physically as a tightening in the chest, a knot in the solar plexus, or stomach pains, or just vaguely experienced as a sort of cloud, emotions get our attention quickly. Unfortunately, they tend to be rather vapid, easily manipulated, rapidly changing, and often undifferentiated. On being asked, many people know that they have a lot of feelings—they just don't know which ones.

We actually like to have our emotions manipulated. If this were not so, the cinema industry would go out of business very quickly. We watch movies in order to have our emotions engaged and then manipulated. This we experience as entertainment, but it cannot be said to be a very profound experience. The same is true of reading and listening to music (of all sorts, from classical to hard rock)—even "serious" entertainment is a shallow experience compared with being present in the heart. Ultimately, all entertainment is a distraction, offered as a sacrifice of reality to appease an ever-hungry mind. In its turn, the mind is constantly striving to lessen the importance of the present moment by seeking out distraction. When we feed that process, we are encouraging that which is most destructive within us.

In particular, emotion is of little importance in establishing or developing our contact with God, and yet almost everyone alive is tempted to use emotion in just that way. Unfortunately, this makes the presence of God nothing more important than a feeling, on a level with being happy or sad. Moreover, if our concept of worship is simply one of distraction—if our conscious contact with God is not radically different from our experience in a theater or an auditorium—then the mind has won a decisive battle. God is then exiled to the past or the future, where He is totally powerless—He is completely at the mercy of the human mind which imprisons Him there.

Since the mind concerns itself with the future and the past, it follows that the mind is also dependent on time. According to the best and brightest, this "fourth dimension" is something of a mystery in itself and cannot be described in any way that is altogether satisfactory. However, within time one thing is certain: everything that exists now has come into being at some point in the past, and everything that exists now is going to cease to exist at some point in the future. This places the mind in a very uncomfortable position: within the dimension in which it chooses to operate, its own destruction is inevitable. For the mind, fear of death, of total destruction, is a constant companion.

In fallen humanity, the mind and the heart have been alienated from each other. The heart has been almost entirely hidden from view, or at least obscured. The mind has started to function on its own, separately from the heart. It actually has the audacity to set up shop on its own and start behaving as if it had a life of its own. This is where the problems start. The mind is very good and valuable as a tool, but it does not have the strength of character to be independent.

It is as if a person has a personal computer he uses for all his work: correspondence, appointments, contacts, finances, and whatnot. One day the computer goes on the Internet and starts to communicate with others as if it were the person who owns it—as if a computer of mine were able to get on the Internet and converse with other people, calling itself Father Meletios. This is almost exactly what the human mind has done. Estranged from the heart, the mind has set up an independent operation; it begins to act with a sense of independence which, if unchecked, ultimately brings ruin and destruction to everything it touches.

Why is this process so destructive? The answer lies mainly in the way the mind is set up to operate. The mind is the great defense system we need to process all the information we receive. However, in so doing, the mind is self-centered, judgmental, and fearful of attack. It expects and assumes the worst from the world, from other people, and ultimately from God. Every detail in the universe is measured by the mind against its usefulness to the mind's story of the self, the ego. The mind attempts to replace the real center of being, the heart, with a center of its own creation.

The mind is judgmental in everything it does. To demonstrate this point, I often recommend an exercise that consists in taking notice of people (although not in such a way as to make them feel uncomfortable). The catch is to notice people without mentally labeling them in any way. Sit quietly at an airport or a bus terminal and notice people without giving them any labels. It is actually quite a difficult thing to do. As we walk down a crowded street, those people we notice are labeled one by one, and often not in the most flattering manner. The ones we ignore are implicitly labeled as unworthy of a label.

It is as if we attempt to deal with each person as a threat or challenge. "Too small, too fat, too good-looking . . ." But in so doing, we also dismiss the people as individuals. "You have your label—I have summed you up—now go away." Having given each person a label, we then feel free to pass on to the next, as if labeling actually made them, in some sense, ours.

The purpose of the exercise is to get to a point where we can notice a person without giving him or her a label. At that point we can begin to experience true compassion—indeed, to see that person as God sees him or her. The less inclination there is to label (which defines people and sets them apart), the more intense is the love—a love that goes in both directions at once, both to and from the person being noticed. This is a very powerful experience.

Another useful exercise, which tests both the strength of our honesty and the degree of our willingness, is to read the words of Jesus in the Gospels slowly, listening first with the mind (in the normal way), and then from a place of great stillness. Get hold of a copy of the New Testament that highlights the words of Jesus in red.[3] Much of what Jesus says (for example, "Love your enemies" or "Blessed are the pure in heart") will be condemned by our minds as dangerous nonsense. In fact (if we are honest with ourselves), if the words of the Gospel do not make our minds feel very uncomfortable every time we hear them, we are not listening hard enough. Receiving the words in a place of great stillness, however, gives the teachings a new dimension, one we might learn to recognize as being separate from the mind. The heart receives the words of Jesus with quiet joy.

Take care, though, not to have any expectations of what should happen, and don't make the mistake of assuming that you might receive some sort of personal revelation. As with everything to do with the heart, all that is to be gained from this exercise is a subtle awareness—an awareness that is rich and fulfilling, but also deeply personal. It makes us alive to a possibility; that is all.

---

3   *The Orthodox Study Bible* (Nashville, TN: Thomas Nelson Publishers, 1993) is very suitable for this exercise.

Today we have more time to dwell on our problems than our ancestors ever did. Our free time, whether in old age (now greatly extended) or simply between tasks, is dominated by a hundred and one distractions, often organized to take place one after the other. Thus, when we do get a free moment, the thoughts in our heads think that nothing is happening and want to move on quickly to something more pressing. This leaves us with a feeling of "lack of fulfillment" which some people actually mistake for life itself, when in fact it is simply the chattering of the mind. It is no more life itself than the exhaust of a bus is the bus itself.

Finally, there is one more aspect of the mind which is commonly experienced, and which has a tremendous effect on a person's spiritual development. The mind lives in a realm in which everything that is known has to have an opposite. "Up" must have a "down," "good" must have a "bad." The energy of the mind consists in comparison: "I" with "not-I," this experience with that experience, this word with that word. The mind sees everything in contrast, valuing differences and ignoring identity.

We may be forgiven for thinking that this is the normal state of things. However, it is worth considering that Jesus often used terms in a way that makes it plain that they have no opposites. "I have come that they may have life, and that they may have *it* more abundantly" (John 10:10). Here, as in other places, Jesus is not referring to life as the opposite of death. Nor, indeed, is He talking about life in any quantitative fashion; having life "abundantly" has something to do with quality, not quantity. Quantity belongs to the mind. Issues of quality belong to the heart.

It is probably fair to say that in the Kingdom Jesus came to proclaim, words like "life," "peace," and "joy" have no opposites. As one contemporary spiritual teacher has said, "The opposite of death is not life; life has no opposite. The opposite of death is birth."

ᚃ THE HEART ᚄ

The doings of the mind are easy to talk about. When it comes to describing the heart, words begin to fail, and the experience of silence becomes more and more important. There is no rightness or wrongness here. Here there is simply awareness.

It is probably appropriate to say that the heart is quiet rather than noisy, intuitive rather than deductive, lives entirely in the present, and is, at every moment, accepting of the reality God gives in that moment. Moreover, the heart does not seek to distance or dominate anything or anyone by labeling. Rather, it begins with an awareness of its relationship with the rest of creation (and everything and everyone in it), accepting rather than rejecting, finding similarity rather than alienation and likeness rather than difference. It knows no fear, experiences no desire, and never finds the need to defend or justify itself. Unlike the mind, the heart never seeks to impose itself. It is patient and undemanding. Little wonder, then, that the mind, always impatient and very demanding, manages to dominate it so thoroughly.

Further, one might guess that the heart is capable of constant awareness of God, and we can see that awareness, albeit in a weakened state, whenever we quiet the mind long enough to hear the silence. The heart functions at an altogether more profound level than the mind, achieving states of awareness and experience far removed from the tyranny of the logismoi or the vanity of emotion.

The heart experiences the Kingdom of heaven, although at this time in the fallen state, in shadow rather than in light. Within the Kingdom there is no time, simply eternity—or more plainly, only "now." Within the Kingdom, identity is treasured, not difference. The very atmosphere of the Kingdom is love and life and peace, and these have no opposites: they are absolute. They are the love of God, eternal life, and the peace of God which is beyond understanding.

The language of the heart is silence—not a bleak, empty silence, but a profound and meaningful silence that ceaselessly sings the glory of God.

While present in all human beings, the heart lies hidden and barely functions in most people most of the time. In one of our liturgical texts it is described as a beautiful mirror covered in dust. Sometimes there is so much dust that it seems as if the heart does not exist at all, but at other times the action of prayer starts to brush the dust away, revealing the glory that lies beneath. The cleaner the mirror, the more polished it is, the more clearly it reflects the glory of God. Once we start to clean the mirror—which is, essentially, the work of prayer—then the mirror slowly comes into view, the dust is gently swept away from its surface, and the light can shine once more.

While the mind often behaves as if the heart did not exist (indeed, it often behaves as if nothing else existed), the heart keeps a very close watch on the mind, acting as a hidden guardian, compensating and mending where possible, ministering, loving, nurturing. The mind perhaps knows this to be the case, but seems not to care. How often the heart is the only factor that saves the human person from total catastrophe is a matter that can only be discerned by the individual.

As with the Prophet Elias (Elijah), part of our spiritual path is to come to an awareness that God is not in the earthquake, the wind, or the fire, where we expect Him to be. God is in the sound of silence (1 Kings 19:12). We listen to this silence by becoming intensely aware, intensely present, and we become intensely present by listening to the silence. The Fathers use the word *nepsis* for this state—a sense of being completely ready, completely alert, totally conscious. When we are lost in thought (so often mistaken for a deeply prayerful state), we are not alert, present, or aware. We cannot be any of those things until we go beyond the mind, seeking a deeper and yet deeper silence indicative of the presence of God.

❦ FINDING HEALING ❧

The purpose and aim of the spiritual life is to allow God to heal us. This opportunity presents itself in many forms and for many reasons. The major rift between the body and the person is healed, by God's grace, through participation in the Holy Mysteries of the Church. The rift between the heart and the mind is healed through "ascetic labor"—prayerful effort—which begins with making the mind quiet, and ends with wrapping the mind and the emotions in prayer and placing them in the heart, where they rightfully belong and where their final integration takes place.

Viewed in another light, our spiritual path leads us toward a state the Fathers called *apatheia*, "passionlessness." This state is the goal of prayer and is experienced as something spontaneous, innocent, and simple. *Apatheia* does not mean "apathetic" (which would be the interpretation of the mind), but free and giving and loving (attributes that find resonance in the heart).

To sum up our discussion thus far, three major themes may prove useful to those who are on any spiritual path:

1 **THE MIND,** the source of the logismoi, creates an awareness of a shallow, or sometimes a false, sense of self. The story or drama with which this shallow self concerns itself throughout life is, collected together, the ego of that particular person. Because of the Fall, this sense of self is broken. Although it mimics reality, it is actually an invention of the individual person and not real at all. Beautiful and necessary when used voluntarily, the mind also functions in an involuntary mode the rest of the time. These involuntary workings of the mind need, most often, to be brushed aside and made quiet. At the beginning of the process, we may feel very unsure of our new surroundings, since it is actually normal for us to depend on the mind to guide us through life. On learning to put the mind aside, or rather, only to use it when it is needed, one comes to a level of awareness that may be entirely new.

2 **A DEEPER SELF,** in many ways a more real self, is to be found in what the Fathers variously call the heart, the nous, or the soul. This key element is often hidden and almost always ignored in the Western world. However, it is through this nous that we have the capacity for direct contact with God, or, in the words of St. John Chrysostom, the possibility of finding the gate to the Kingdom of heaven.

3 **EMOTION AND FEELING** belong to the mind, not the heart. In many cases, they are simply the body's reaction to thought—a physical accompaniment to the logismoi. While providing a great deal of color to everyday life, emotions and feelings belong to that part of us that needs healing. Since they are always

reactive (feelings do not occur spontaneously, but only in reaction to thought), and since they come originally from the body, not the mind, there is some reason to say that should a comparison be necessary, feelings are probably a little more reliable than thoughts. However, it is not true that they, any more than dreams, always know best or can always be relied on.

Even though the mind and the heart are completely estranged and their functions in our lives completely different, they actually need each other. In the process of falling from the natural grace of God, they became somehow disconnected, even lost to each other. In the practice of Orthodox living they are given the opportunity to stop hurting, to heal, and to start the process of reintegration. Both heart and mind are called to participate in the Mystery which is the life of God, reflected in participation in the Mysteries which are the life of the Church.

~: CHAPTER 2 :~

Orthodoxy— A Relationship with God

Christianity is not a philosophy, not a doctrine, but life.

—ARCHIMANDRITE SOPHRONY

THE ORTHODOX CHURCH IS NOT PRIMARILY AN INSTI-tution. Orthodox Christianity is not a series of rules to live by, nor is it a particular structure of church government. Orthodoxy is not a theological system, nor is its fullest expression limited to any particular period of history or cultural environment.

Orthodoxy is nothing less than a relationship with God.

Of course, the Orthodox Church does have a structure, a structure that exists partly as a living expression of its interpretation of the commandments of Christ, and partly as a result of the various developments that have occurred during the last two thousand years of history. Orthodoxy certainly looks like a religion, but that label is only important when comparing it with the details of other religions. Indeed, there will always be a temptation for us to identify Orthodoxy with other institutions and human systems that we know. However, Orthodoxy is not made better or worse by such a comparison; as a path of spiritual development it stands alone.

Although the Orthodox Church is sometimes seen in terms of an institution, and can, in her less glorious moments, actually behave like one, in essence it is something altogether different from a society, a club, an association, a university, a pressure group, a political party, or a corporation. Finally, even though Orthodoxy does have rules—so many that there is little chance anyone could observe them all—the essential and central experience of Orthodoxy is never in observing all the rules.

At a profound and instinctive level, the Orthodox Church recognizes herself as the Body of Christ. With that in mind, Orthodoxy is the expression of the way God interacts with His people. In other words, Orthodoxy is the way God relates to the Church as the Body of Christ, the way He relates to each individual within it, and conversely a way by which people may interact and interrelate with God.

It may be that in the vast expanses of time and space of our universe, there are many ways of expressing the relationship between the individual and God. Indeed, there may be quite diverse, yet entirely authentic, ways of forming that relationship. However, for those people who call the Orthodox Church home, there exists an awareness, both implicit and explicit in the life of the Church, that this particular relationship between God and His people has a unique quality, and far from being an optional extra to life in general it is, in an essential manner, life itself.

The key to that life is mystery. Mystery is the space where we meet God.

↜ DEVELOPING A RELATIONSHIP WITH GOD ↝

Orthodoxy begins at or before birth, and it does so as an impersonal relationship between a Creator and His creature. However, when the person participates in the Mystery of Holy Baptism, that relationship enters a new dimension: it becomes personal. In a personal relationship, each person has a name and is recognized when called by that name. Jesus talks about this when He says that He, the shepherd, calls His sheep by name, and they recognize His voice. In the Mystery of Baptism, just as the person dies and rises again in the water,

God's name is revealed, but so too is the name of the person being baptized. God now has a way of getting our attention: He can call us by name.

Since the Mystery of Baptism often takes place in early childhood, the young person's awareness of this relationship may not be particularly vivid. In childhood, the whole of life is a mystery, and the relationship with God is just one part of that. Awareness of it may lie dormant for a number of years. However, when the difficulties of life become a more challenging reality, this relationship starts to become more usable, more real, more demanding. In ways great and small, the individual begins to hear the call to repentance, the eternal silent call of a loving God, which invites him or her to respond through a lifetime of transformation and growth.

Naturally, the person is likely to focus on this process at certain moments more than others; yet gradually, often in the background, there occurs an exploration and deepening of his or her feelings and thoughts about God. These thoughts and feelings can be strong or weak, positive or negative, but at some point the person realizes that they are not the whole picture. Simultaneously, and almost always unconsciously, the person also grows in inner awareness in the depths of his or her heart. There, in a space beyond thought and feeling, he or she experiences a silently worded expression of a very real and eternal relationship with God.

As long as life lasts, the person is called towards God and, for better or worse, a steady transformation occurs. It would be nice to say that this transformation is always positive, but that is not the case. If the fears and desires of the person's mind prove to be too strong for the silent witness of the heart, the transformation can be towards paranoia and despair. Moreover, the sinful and unworthy characteristics of the human personality ebb and flow over time, changing direction and focus, sometimes weaker, sometimes stronger. Inevitably, this means that there is growth in some areas, not in others; sometimes improvement, sometimes deterioration.

What one needs to remember, particularly when the path seems very tough and one wonders if it has any value at all, is that the one area where the person is making progress all the time is in experience.

Whether a particular battle is lost or won, there is always the experience, and ultimately this experience leads to progress—although it does not necessarily arrive at anything like perfection in this lifetime. We must be careful to avoid having high expectations of our own performance, while at the same time enjoying as a certainty a high expectation of what God can do. The words of Jesus, "You shall be perfect, just as your Father in heaven is perfect" (Matthew 5:48), do not include a timeline. We will falter, take wrong turns, and make large numbers of mistakes long before reaching anything like perfection.

Ultimately, the human person is drawn into God Himself. This is what the Fathers call *theosis*. In Orthodoxy this is no far-off goal reserved for the few; it is actually very near, and it is for everyone, even though few may realize its tremendous power. It is the everyday expression of the fullness of the Kingdom of heaven, always present in its potential, eternal, always reachable, and not just glimpsed, but actually realized through participation in the mysterious life of God, which is brought to life in the sacred Mysteries of the Church.

❧ RELATIONSHIP AND IDENTITY ☙

Before we can explore the theme of relationship in any meaningful way, it is necessary to examine the theme of identity.

Identity is a form of labeling, something the mind loves to do and which it starts doing when we are still very young. In the fallen world, we are initially aware of ourselves not in some abstract existential sense, but in the form the mind, with its attendant thought patterns, presents to us: I am who I am because I have a unique experience of wanting and fearing. This state of mind can be observed even in very small children. In our earliest personal memories, we notice that it is this small "wanting and fearing" thing that we identify as self, as "I."

Some psychological systems call this entity the "ego," but the experience of Orthodoxy suggests that to do so would be to give it too much reality. It is preferable to reserve that term for the overall shape of the thoughts and feelings that are constantly buzzing around our minds, almost always centered around wanting and fearing—the logismoi. Over time, the logismoi organize themselves into a story, or at least a story-outline, and it is this story which we can identify as the ego. It has no existence of itself; it is simply the shape of a mass of thoughts and feelings. From childhood on, we put almost all our available energy into building and defending this shape or story-line. This life-story stresses the separateness of the person who knows himself as "I want." We can witness it in operation in a person who does not want to share his toys at the age of two, or his financial resources at the age of forty-two.

As we have seen, however, there is another way of sensing oneself, through the heart. The heart neither wants nor fears. Its behavior is not self-centered, since it does not see itself as being under threat, and it is also more trusting than the mind.

In the silent awareness of the nous lie the beginnings of the renewed, spiritually developed person. Here are the seeds of "I am" rather than "I want," an "I am" that is nevertheless aware of its connectedness with God and with the rest of the universe. The person who experiences life through the nous, even fleetingly, is capable of accepting the reality God presents to her or him in any given moment. This is something the mind can never fully do.

People who are able, albeit briefly, to live in (or through) their heart, rather than their mind, experience life from a place of great stillness. They find their feelings of alienation, loneliness, and the desperate need for certainty which accompanies their normal life just drop away. They find themselves capable of relating in a positive way to the universe around them, but they also relate positively to the other "I am's" with whom they share it. A sense of fierce, self-centered competition, which is normal in our fallen world, gives way to a deeper sense of interdependence, cooperation, and trust. Ultimately, too, the "I am" of individuality meets the "I AM" (Exodus 3:14) of divinity, and the former recognizes the latter both as its source and as its goal. It is precisely here that the words of the God-man bring a whole universe into focus: "Before Abraham was, I AM" (John 8:58).

The mind, in contrast, seeks to isolate us and causes us to define ourselves in terms of being different. Most sectarian behavior, in which we all indulge to a greater or lesser extent, has its roots in a system whereby the force of not-belonging to a particular group is actually stronger than any sense of belonging. We identify ourselves most clearly by being quite sure who we are not.[4]

However, this is not the whole story. If it were, there would be no spiritual life, no sense of goodness, joy, generosity, or peace. We would live in a world without love. The heart knows that the sense of alienation emanating from the mind which is experienced by most people is a real enough feeling, but that it is not the whole picture. By listening to their heart, individuals become aware that, in order to be complete, they need to enter relationships. Orthodox theology is very eloquent in this matter: we are more precisely who we are when we are "in communion."[5] This is true from physical birth to physical death, but is limited by neither. Human beings need to be in relationship. This factor may often remain hidden, but the mind eventually fails in its attempt to obscure it altogether. In time and in many ways, the heart's silent desire for relationship is eventually heard.

The situation is somewhat complicated by the fact that the mind thinks it knows what relationship is. However, the concept it imagines is actually on a completely different level. For the mind, a relationship is a chance for the ego to impose its views on someone else. It involves defining who is superior and who is inferior, together with the gross assumption that it is the task of the superior to control the inferior. The mind seeks to make the other an object, an "it," since it does not accept that the other person is as much of a person (with his or her own needs) as the self. Many relationships stay at this point forever. We can see it in the way governments treat individuals, in the way doctors sometimes treat their patients, and in the way all of us tend to treat people from groups quite unlike our own. These "objects"

---

4 An example: A boy plays football for his school team. His loyalty to his own team may exist and may be strong, but it is always somewhat lessened by the fact that he does not like some of the other members, he has scores to settle with some, and he may fear others. His relationship with the opposing team is a much simpler affair. He knows, without thinking about it, that he does not belong to them.

5 The works of Metropolitan John (Zizioulas) of Pergamon are very informative in this matter.

may have names, but it is not important that we know or use them, since they are not completely human to us (at least, not in the sense in which we are completely human to ourselves). The universe is full of things and people who are "it" just by virtue of being "not-me." Most of them remain, for the rest of our lives, nothing more than objects.

From time to time, the mind of an individual may become aware of a type of being which is a sort of supreme "Not-me," and, at least as far as the mind can stretch, is understood as the ultimate source of all the other "not-me's." Having started as a hypothesis ("what if" being one of the mind's favorite games), this Being can gradually become transformed in the mind of the individual until it takes the shape of something like God, a god, a Creator, or some other expression of more or less absolute power.

As awareness of that power grows in the personality, so too does awareness that this Being is other and unlike, even unlike all the other "not-me's" in the Universe. As a result, the individual gradually arrives at a somewhat vague concept that he or she (or, more precisely, his or her ego) is not the driving force of the universe, but that something or someone else is. By becoming more distinctly aware that he himself is "not-God," the individual instinctively moves towards God, who is power and Creator. God exists, God is present, and it is possible to relate to Him—but at this level He is a force, a power. This is the mind's version of a relationship.

It is not easy to have a relationship with a force.

❧ RELATING TO GOD AS PERSON OR POWER ☙

The whole issue of the difference between having a relationship with a person and having a relationship with a power is of crucial importance and requires a little more exploration.

God, when regarded as Creator of heaven and earth, is not obviously personal, any more than a nuclear explosion is personal. Here He is in the abstract—a power; even the pronoun "He" is hardly merited. Much more than a physical presence, He is seen as all-present, all-knowing, all-powerful, and, in a word, perfect. Naturally, if this perfection is real, He stays the same, since perfection cannot be improved on. In this aspect, God is an "It." He is as unapproachable and as immovable as the universe around us which He has created.

It is possible to enter into a relationship with pure power, but the resulting relationship tends to be one-sided, more like that between a master and his slave. The slave's knowledge of the master is limited. He is trained to act on orders without questioning them, to obey without scrutiny. Many relationships with God look like exactly that. People who have this sort of relationship with God talk a lot about right and wrong and tend to have a black-and-white view of life. They are usually happy only when other people share their view of life, the universe, and God Himself. Many of the religious systems in the world mirror this type of relationship.

If we regard God merely as a power, we tend to project onto Him the task of providing us with a source of the things we want to hold as absolutes in an ever-changing world. The god of philosophy is naturally "good." He is not only good, but is "the Good" by which we judge all other persons and things—something the mind, unlike the heart, is very keen to do. However, there is a problem here. Very often our idea of what good is depends on our situation,[6] and we are again in danger of making something out of God which is not God, but is of our own imaginings.

The God who is merely the source of moral absolutes is likely to be a disappointment whenever we face a problem that does not have a clear answer. There is no room for negotiation with an absolute force, nowhere to exercise our personal freedom.

A person who is in relationship with a power alone is not a whole person, since there is no communion. Personhood comes about when the person of one being enters into relationship with the person of another being. Relationship always entails growth, and growth implies change. If there is no growth in a relationship, there is no development as a person either. In fact, if there is no growth in this

---

6 What is "good" for you may not be "good" for me. The fine sunny weather that is good for me while I am lying on the beach having a vacation is not good for the farmer two miles away whose crops are dying for lack of water. The burglar might have a good night if he successfully raids six houses. Yet, the same event is hardly good for the people whose houses have been robbed.

relationship with God, the human person actually diminishes, since it is unnourished. The power that is understood to be God inevitably becomes more distant, a more unrelated force.

A person who is in a relationship is forced to put his or her life to the test, to come into judgment through the presence of the "other." We cannot do that with a power as such; we simply comply, or fail or refuse to comply, with the commands the power gives us. So long as we relate to God merely as a power, He is stuck in the category of an "object" to whom we cannot relate. Only when we relate to God as a person can we grow "into" God.

ᴄ: RELATIONSHIP AND THE FALL :ᴐ

When we relate to God as an object or a thing, our greatest hope for advancement lies in rebellion. This is what we see happening in the first two chapters of the Bible. At the beginning of this story, the man and the woman were in a beautiful relationship with God. The relationship was loving and nurturing, and the young couple found God full of tenderness and compassion; they even went for walks with Him in the evening. However, something in them started to go wrong, and they made a move which to them looked like a bid for freedom. The sad part is, they were already free—they just didn't know it.

They were tempted by the notion of getting something for nothing, without effort. "Eat the apple and all will be well," they were told. Instead of making slow and steady progress in relationship (often involving a great deal of work), as a child makes with its parents, as friends or lovers make together, the man and the woman both decided to avoid growth and the slow progress of relationship-building. Instead, they went straight for what looked like the major prize, the godlike status of knowledge. It is particularly interesting in the context of this book that they were offered knowledge (the domain of the mind) and not wisdom (the domain of the heart).

What the tempter actually offered them was the knowledge we call discernment—how to tell good from bad. Here, in story form, we are shown the origins of our apparent need to label things, to judge things. Their decision looked good from their standpoint, since it appeared to give them freedom of choice, and that was attractive. Adam and Eve wanted that freedom, but they were too young, too immature, to take the responsibility that went along with it. They thought they could get freedom without responsibility. Only an adult knows there is no such thing.

God did not kill the man and the woman (which shows that God does not operate on the level of the human mind). What He did was to alter their reality so that they became aware of their separateness, their estrangement, from God, who until then had been their sole purpose for being. The man and the woman rejected relationship with God as a person and went into exile. They forced God to become an impersonal power, a demand, a commandment, just as a rebellious child forces a parent to become overpowering, impersonal, and free from dialogue when the child presses beyond the limits that have been provided for its safety and nurture.

According to the thoughts that course through the human mind, the situation that emerges at the end of the story of Adam and Eve is considered to be the end of the whole story. Certainly this situation is reflected in the attitudes of contemporary society. God is a "take-it-or-leave-it" sort of thing, useful if manipulated, otherwise merely the relic of a bygone, unsophisticated age. This distant yet powerful God depends on logic and human interest to exist at all. Ultimately God is merely something or someone unknown but very powerful. Like children with their hands over their eyes, humanity can "unmake" God by covering their sight, thereby not only depriving themselves of the source of their lives, but emerging with a lack of the one thing they deem God capable of providing—an absolute sense of right and wrong.

Where there is power, there will always be human beings who like to wield it for their own ends. Throughout history, individuals have realized there is an advantage to be gained by persuading other people that they have this "God-power" under their control. This has been the normal function of religion in almost all civilizations, and it is demonstrated in a number of ways. Since, in this context, God is merely a force or a power, people try to control it, predict the mind of the power, or even foretell what the power is going to do next. They force the power to limit itself in one way or another, either making itself available only in a given form (in or through a particular interpretation of a scripture or revelation), or allowing it to function only through the intermediary of a priesthood, an infallible spokesperson, or a particular human institution. In the end such a religion becomes yet another way of manipulating people so that the few can control the many to benefit their own political, social, or financial aspirations.

These last few sentences are a fairly harsh judgment of what religion has meant to most people throughout most of our history. In fact, this is precisely what religion looks like when it is controlled by the ways of the fallen human mind. Since the mind fears uncertainty, it is natural that, at this level, religion is used as a means of gaining certainty in an uncertain universe, as well as allowing some people to impose their own wants and desires on others in the name of their deity. If those with power label this certainty as "faith," they may think they have achieved their goal. However, this is not the case. Faith does not exist in the mind. It exists in the heart. And even in the heart, it is always a gift from God, not a conclusion of the mind's computation. In its fallen state, the best the mind can offer by way of faith is simply a strongly held opinion. "Strongly held opinion" describes prejudice, not faith.

We cannot make an opinion, even a strongly held opinion, sacrosanct by labeling it "faith" and then behaving for all the world as if it could not be challenged. To do so is to belittle genuine faith—which comes not as a result of thinking but as a result of trusting God—and to place our own needs as the driving force of the universe. If we need to be certain about anything, let it not be about our own fears and desires. If we are busy defending God, we can be fairly sure we are stuck in our minds. In the domain of the heart, truth never needs a defense.

The desire to be certain manifests itself in another, more perverse and dangerous quality: the need to be right. The thinking goes like this: If I am right, I can impose my worldview (my fears and desires) on other people with impunity. In the religious world, there is another benefit: If I can subscribe to a religious tradition that is right, my own personal shortcomings (together with my fears and insecurities) seem less important, and I can pretend to exist at a level of certainty which normal reality denies me.

There is something else here we need to notice. In order to be right about anything, the mind has the need to find someone or something that is wrong. In a sense, the mind is always looking for an enemy (the person who is "wrong"), since without an enemy, the mind is not quite sure of its own identity. When it has an enemy, it is able to be more confident about itself. Since the mind also continually seeks for certainty, which is a by-product of the desire to be right, the process of finding and defining enemies is an ongoing struggle for survival. Declaring enemies is, for the mind, not an unfortunate character flaw, but an essential and necessary task.

Unfortunately, being right is not what people really need, even though a great deal of their lives may be taken up in its pursuit. Defense of the ego is almost always a matter of trying to be right. Interestingly enough, Jesus never once suggested to His disciples that they be right. What He did demand is that they be righteous. In listening to His words we find that we spend almost all our energy in the wrong direction, since we generally pursue being right with every ounce of our being, but leave being good to the weak and the naïve.

People fight wars, commit genocide, and deprive others of basic human civil liberties, all in the name of being right. There is little doubt that if a further nuclear war ever takes place, it will be because the person pushing the button believes himself to be right. About *something*.

Religion, at the level of the mind, can be a terrible thing, causing wanton destruction to individuals, families, and even entire nations, all in the cause of being right. Almost every religious system can, and in most cases, has operated solely at this level at some point in its history. This is the level of religious awareness that can cause the servants of the King of Peace to wage war on those who think thoughts different from their own; it bestows on those who have been commanded to forgive their enemies the right to annihilate their foes.

Happily this is not the whole situation, and the experience of the Orthodox Church maintains that there is indeed another level of awareness—experienced not by the mind, but by the heart—that gives a much fuller, often complementary, view of what reality is all about, including our own religious experience.

~: HUMANITY AND DIVINITY MEET :~

Like the prodigal son in the parable, when we turn to God we expect Him to be impersonal, to treat us as an employer might treat us. If it is true that our minds seek a God who is little more than a supreme source of power, the experience of Orthodoxy points to God wanting to approach us in a completely different way.

Metropolitan Anthony Bloom, one of the most outstanding spiritual leaders of the twentieth century, tells us what the relationship with God is like:

Have another look at the passage in The Little Prince *by Antoine de Saint-Exupéry where the fox describes how the little prince should learn to tame him—he must be very patient, sit a little way off and look at him out of the corner of his eye and say nothing, for words cause misunderstandings. And every day he will sit a little closer and they will become friends. Put "God" in the place of the fox and you will see loving, chaste shyness, a diffidence which offers but does not prostitute itself: God does not accept a glib, smooth relationship, nor does he impose his presence—he offers it, but it can only be received on the same terms, those of a humble, loving heart, when two timidly, shyly seeking people reach to each other because of a deep mutual respect and because both recognize the holiness and the extraordinary beauty of reciprocal love.*[7]

Through the Incarnation of our Lord and God and Savior, Jesus Christ, the whole scheme of relationship with God that had existed up until that moment of history was broken down and built up again in a completely different manner. With the Incarnation of the Son of God, the God-man Jesus Christ became the unique bridge between

---

7 Metropolitan Anthony Bloom, *Meditations: A Spiritual Journey through the Parables* (Denville, NJ: Dimension Books, 1971), pp. 26–27.

the individual person, with his or her strong experience of being a separate self, and the God of heaven. This is no mere theory. With the Incarnation, God is no longer simply a power, but a Person with a name. That name is "Father." It is possible to have a relationship with Father in a way that is never possible with Power. Having met the Son, we know the Father, and we know both through the action of the Holy Spirit.

We have always had the possibility of a relationship with the Power who is the Creator of the universe, but now we can also voluntarily enter a relationship with God who chooses to "lower Himself" sufficiently for us to enter into a personal relationship with Him. What was closed to Adam and Eve through the exercise of their own choice is now open and available to us. And it is not simply returning to the situation Adam and Eve enjoyed. We are not invited to return to our prefallen condition (although that in itself would be miraculous). Rather, we are invited to enter into a level of intimacy with God that was not available to our first parents.

This new, voluntary relationship, the immediate person-to-person relationship with God, is difficult to sustain in everyday life. When a couple decides to get married, they want to see each other every moment of every day for the first few weeks. (Whether this is because of fear or desire does not really matter, since both reflect the influence of the mind.) As time goes on, they gradually become accustomed to allowing each other more independence, and each gets to a point where he or she regains a sort of autonomy, although they know that at a significant level they trust each other completely. This newly found independence is quite different from their state of independence before the marriage started, since it is based on trust and not merely on a fear of being isolated.

The relationship with God as a person is very similar. Sometimes we want to feel independent. Sometimes we hate to be left alone. There are times when closeness seems to be very necessary and other times when estrangement seems to be in order. We have to expect that, from time to time, God appears to want to pull away from the relationship as much as we do.

Some of the greatest spiritual writers have experienced the stark awareness of the absence of God at times in their lives. This experience is easily as strong, and sometimes much more long-lasting, than any ecstatic awareness of God's presence they may have at other times. Yet this sense of God's absence seems to be part of the overall picture, and we need to learn to accept those times just as much as those at the other end of the spectrum—those times when, without warning, we are suddenly totally aware of the intensity of our relationship with God.

While it seems necessary that God take the initiative in opening Himself to us, we cannot expect Him to take complete control of how the relationship develops. As in any friendship, if one partner dominates too much, we do not have a relationship at all. This is one of our most common mistakes in approaching God. It is an axiom that God, as a power, is all-knowing, all-seeing, all-hearing, and so on, but in addition, we have a tendency to think, "Well, if You are so good at everything, why not just take over?" But that is not what God seeks. He seeks a response, a voluntary offering of the open heart, not the automatic response of a robot. We cannot have a love affair with a robot. Neither can He.

∼: GOD'S DESIRE FOR RELATIONSHIP :∼

Throughout the Old Testament, we see God showing signs of wanting to be in relationship. He obviously enjoyed the company of some of His creatures: Noah, Abraham, and the other patriarchs. He chose His friends not because He was the Creator of heaven and earth, although that was, of course, true. He chose His friends in a way that suggests He wanted to enter a more genuine relationship.

In much the same way, a king might be busy being a king all the time, but sometimes he just wants to get together with his friends and have some fun. The friends might be reasonably careful not to overstep the boundaries of the king's friendship—after all, he remains the king, and certain niceties have to be observed. Nevertheless, in the core of his friendship, the king has no more power than anyone else. If the king wants someone to love him, to trust him and respect him for his own sake, he must be prepared to open up sufficiently to allow his friends to be fully human and fully free. He has to take the risk of being rejected.

God takes risks. The Incarnation of Jesus was perhaps the greatest risk ever taken.

In making genuine relationships, there always has to be a certain amount of risk-taking. For example, if I want to relate to you, I have to lay myself open to you, even if ever so slightly, and I may hope that in return you will take the risk of laying yourself open to me.

That is why rejection hurts so much, and why we justifiably avoid it as often as possible. If I show you who I really am, at a level that is usually closed to other people, I stand the risk of you looking at me and deciding that you would rather not bother. Then I am rejected. It sometimes happens that rejection is so terrible that a person refuses to open himself up to anyone ever again. In that case it has become a mental sickness and usually needs professional help. However, no matter how dangerous it looks, taking risks in order to make relationships is fundamental to being human.

To say that God takes risks is not to belittle His Being. Certainly, to talk of God "needing" something or someone makes little sense. However, God shows His true greatness when He shows His ability to be weak. To condescend—to get down to our level—is the way God makes Himself open to us. And by doing so, He makes Himself vulnerable, just as we make ourselves vulnerable to the influence of others when we want to get to know them better.

God knows us better than we know ourselves. He knows how many hairs we have on our head, according to the words of Jesus, and that is rather better than we know ourselves, each other, or even someone we love very much. He knows our heartbeat and our blood pressure. He knows our moods and our physical status. He knows the workings of our minds with all the attendant desires and wants, needs and disappointments. At the level of Creator, he knows all these things, for there is nothing that exists that does not emanate from the mind of God. It is as if nothing can possibly happen that God has not thought up first. But more than that, He seeks to know us as friends, and friends can hide things from each other.

When God gives us a gift, it is as a result of His generosity and

His own freedom. We accept the gift or reject it. Both the acceptance and the rejection have their roots in our freedom. If we want to give a gift to someone we love, we must have the choice not to give that gift; otherwise the gift is nothing. Generosity always has its grounding in freedom.

That may be what Holy Scripture means when it states that we are made in the image of God. That freedom as "friends" is what makes us like God. If we look at this in a different way, however, we come to realize that this same freedom is precisely the only thing we have to offer God. It is the one thing we have that is entirely dependent on us, since freedom was His gift to us from the beginning, and He does not take His gifts back.

So, at some stages, we have to know God as Creator and be in relationship with an idea, a power, or even an ideal. At a more profound level, we are invited to get to know Him as a Person. This is supremely true when we contemplate the Person of Jesus the Christ and His revelation of the Father and of the Holy Spirit. Part of the automatic identity of each one of us is that God is our Creator. Part of our chosen identity, the part that results from our freedom, is that God is our Father. Using the vocabulary of the Orthodox liturgy, this is called a "dare."[8] It is as if we approach the throne of God, and instead of cringing like prisoners, awaiting the wrath we have earned, we hold up our lives and shout out like small children, "Papa—look!"

In the beginning of his Gospel, St. John gives a summary of the Church's understanding of the Person of Christ, which lies at the heart of all subsequent Orthodox theology. Christ Himself is knowable on many levels, not least as the Word of God through whom creation came to be. But He also took flesh and lived with us around two thousand years ago. It is because Christ became a human person that we can relate to Him, and through Him to the Father.

---

8   Just before the Lord's Prayer in the Divine Liturgy, we hear, "Master, grant that with confidence and without fear, we may dare to call the God of heaven 'Father,' and say: Our Father . . ."

Another area in which the mind has become involved with our spiritual development is in the use of imagination. This provides a potential minefield on those occasions when we use our imagination to invent God before trying to have a relationship with Him.

Children often have imaginary playmates. If you had one, you may remember how real that friend was to you, but how difficult it was to bring the friend into the rest of your life. Your mother and father could not see him or her, and your invisible friend was as likely as not to be sat upon, walked through, or otherwise ignored. The whole process only worked at all because in your mind your friend had a body and all the other things humans have. Your only difficulty was that his or her presence was limited to your imagination. If you stopped imagining, your friend disappeared.

In much the same way, we often concoct images of God in our heads. These images may serve us well for a little while, but after a time it becomes important that we share these images with other human beings, and then the problems begin. A god who is limited by a power of imagination is not a god at all. It may be that I have a false image or idea about God, which changes as I change and grows as I grow, but I cannot meet that god, for it has no existence apart from me. It is ironic, but worthy of note, that one way we can know we are meeting the real God is when He acts in a way we do not understand!

Very often, one of the most painful things adults have to do as parents, educators, and counselors is to invite young people to examine their images of God. Having examined them, they have to destroy them. When we are little, we are often taught about a God who is "meek and mild" and turns out to be more like a grandfather made out of sugar candy than a real person. As we pass from childhood to adolescence, it is important that we get rid of the images of God that will not be of any use in our adult lives. More importantly, we have to stop imagining what God is like and start having a relationship, on that more elevated, personal level, with the God who really is.

We do not need to use our minds to imagine Jesus. In making up an image in our heads, we are making a false idol. I think that is why the Church has never chosen one particular picture of Jesus to be regarded as *the* icon of Christ. The painted icon is a result of the collective awareness of the Church over long periods of time; but there is no icon of which we can say, "This is who Jesus really was," because all icons fall short of the reality.

In the end, our relationship with God does not depend on our artistic capabilities. On the essential level, our relationship with God depends on His approaching us and offering His presence to us.

Parents make the process of learning to know God more difficult for their children whenever they invent or use established imaginary figures (tooth fairy, Easter Bunny, Santa Claus) to provide their children with information, entertainment, or tradition. Unfortunately, they then progressively remove these figures as their children grow up. It is hardly surprising that God tends to be added to that list. Certainly, if He is only a figment of someone's imagination, He deserves to become as extinct as the tooth fairy.

For God to be in any sense real for a person, every aspect of the relationship with God has to be reflected in that person's relationships with other people. We always test the unknown against our experience of the known, even when this "known" is actually a mistake. Our regular experience of life is one of trying to make sense. As very young children, we start to collect information about the world around us, even before we can see the "big picture" that comes with more experience of life. This is why our memories of childhood are often so confusing.

I was born in 1950, and I remember, for example, that my parents often talked about the Second World War, which had not only been a dramatic part of their own growing up, but was also the cause of their meeting. I listened to them talking about the war—a war that started when they were both teenagers—on numerous occasions, since it was by far the most significant feature of their young lives. But it wasn't a feature of mine (if you exclude ration books and bomb sites, which were still common enough in the London of my childhood). Several years later, I came to realize that I had grown up with a misconception. The misconception, unchallenged for a long time, was that everyone experienced a war in his or her late teens. The two most important people in my life, whose view of the world was the foundation for my own, had sown these seeds, although they had no idea that they were conveying this erroneous notion to me.

In the beginning of our relationship with God, there are likely to be some situations we cannot understand, or that lead us to believe erroneous information. This is hardly surprising, since the phenomenon is also encountered when we form relationships with other people; however, we tend to be more forgiving in our relationships with other human beings than in our relationship with God. Even though we test the relationship with God against a pattern of what we have learned in our human relations (for we have no other patterns to test it against), we tend to demand a good deal of God, and often expect a higher standard of cooperation.

We often hear somebody say something like, "I do not like what has happened in this disaster or that; if God existed at all, He would not have allowed it to happen."[9] According to this attitude, God has taken a test and failed; as a result, He has been sent up the river of nonexistence as a punishment. We have a tendency not to give God a chance and to insist that He get it right the first time. There is an absolute quality in God, but it is not found in the way He approaches us—*that* He does in humility and with great diffidence.

∾ ASPECTS OF OUR RELATIONSHIP WITH GOD ∾

When we meet God, we encounter Him at many different levels, and so there are many ways in which we can categorize our relationship. Sometimes we are like a child going to a parent for a cuddle, for a telling-off, or for a little encouragement. Sometimes we are like employees being called to account for some technical quality of life. We often like to dwell on the fact that we are cocreators with God, but so often we simply destroy what He creates. He knows how to make the ecology of a rainforest; we know how to destroy it. He creates life

---

9 Consider the title of a TV show in Britain on Christmas Day, 2005: "Tsunami: Where Was God?"

in the womb with our assistance, but we have the power to stamp out that life. Our power and our responsibility do not always match with His, and in many cases we find ourselves needing to realign the reality we face. A quick meeting, an encounter, a judgment is required to get us back on track.

Sometimes we approach God like a friend, sometimes even like a lover. In these cases, the relationship is much more equal, as both parties are equally vulnerable. If this were not true, love in its fullest sense could not happen. At this level, it is possible to talk about God having extremely human qualities—such as trying something out, or even making mistakes. However, we tend to get nervous around a God who can make mistakes, because our need for control is so great.

Sometimes we have to approach God in a spirit of forgiveness—not because He has done actual wrong, but because He has done something we do not like. Any encounter with God is a judgment; most often it is our condemnation which is involved. However, sometimes the judgment is against God. When we have the courage to call God "Father," we also have to have the courage to forgive God our Father—just as, ultimately, we have to forgive our earthly fathers for being less than they might be. For example, the person who loses a young child, friend, or spouse to death has, at some point, to approach God with a view to forgiving Him. Nothing else will do.

∿ ENTERING THE MYSTERY ∿

In the preceding sections, much has been said about how we are able to approach God as a person, just as we are able to approach a human person and make a relationship with her or him. One aspect of our relationship with God is, however, clearly different.

When we get to know a person, we expect to spend some time learning about their ways, their views, their likes and dislikes, their ups and downs, their weak and their strong points. Eventually, perhaps after many years, we reach a stage at which we do not really expect to find any more surprises in them. We know them. We can even predict what they will do in any given situation.

I remember watching an elderly couple in a café in London many years ago. They were obviously together and were quietly drinking their tea. They exchanged not one word the whole time they were there. It was as if they had already said everything that needed to be said. They sat in complete yet comfortable silence, not even looking at each other.

When we enter a personal relationship with God, we try to go from the unknown to the known, as we do with a human being. However, once we start to function in a spiritual manner, the progression is from the unknown to the more unknown, and yet we keep going willingly and gladly. Here, the capacity of our broken mind is of little or no use, and the heart comes into its own. Words make no sense, and eventually, like the old couple, we come to a stage where there is simply a silence—an eloquent yet comfortable silence. That silence is prayer.

The relationship with God automatically changes and enlivens our relationships with other people and the rest of the created world. As individuals go deeper into the Mystery, deeper into the place of uncertainty, they actually get closer to each other. The rather unsubtle image stuck in my mind is that of the sports stadium. Imagine Christ standing in the middle of the field, calling each person by name to come towards Him. Scattered throughout the stadium, some in the seats near the front, others way off in the bleachers, each person who responds to the call starts to come closer to God; but in so doing, he or she inevitably gets closer to all the other people too. We may, indeed, start in a place of alienation and distrust, but gradually we come to a place of belonging. The closer we are to God, the less alienated we are from other people.

~: CHAPTER 3 :~

Distraction & Prayer

IT SEEMS ODD THAT DURING MUCH OF OUR LIVES, MOST of the time, we seek distraction. Any sort of distraction seems to do, anything that takes us away from the present moment. The mind gravely distrusts the present moment and will do almost anything to get us away from it. This is all the more puzzling when we realize that the present moment is the only moment we have.

Succeeding generations seek different sorts of distractions, and generally each group prefers their own to those popular among those who are younger. We justify our own choices of distraction for all sorts of empty reasons. We love to be lost in thought or to have our emotions tugged. Almost every television show we watch involves the invention, then the resolution, of a tension—a tension whose main purpose is to engage our emotions. But the tension is entirely unreal, entirely unnecessary, and does nothing but kill time, usually in chunks of thirty minutes or an hour, every hour, from late afternoon to late at night, or even longer.

Organized sports are a massive form of distraction. An artificial world is created in which teams struggle for supremacy. Nevertheless, for all its lack of meaning, it provides enough apparent pleasure to enough people that it is almost unthinkable to have a world without sport. Other distractions include reading, running marathons, and sewing, all of which can be quite constructive. We can do things which are obviously good with a view to being distracted. For example, we can go to church to be distracted. Good music, a fine and moving sermon—these can all lead to distraction. It is not uncommon to go to church, find our place, and then attempt to get lost in our thoughts for the next hour and a half. We can do the same in the concert hall, the movie house, or the library. The only difference is that we usually feel a greater sense of satisfaction when we do it in church.

There are "posh" distractions like collecting first editions, listening to Beethoven's late string quartets, enjoying fine wines, and reading Shakespeare for fun. There are not-so-posh distractions like football, roller coasters, and the happy hour at the local bar. However, they are all distractions. They all lead us away from being the person we are and towards attempting to find fulfillment outside ourselves, preferably away from ourselves and certainly away from the present moment.

Distractions contain the seeds of a further danger. If they become the central theme of a person's life, they are likely to become an addiction—a situation in which the person does not have the behavior, but the behavior has the person. When a person seeks himself or herself in drinking or smoking, taking drugs, or any other activity which lends itself to the thought, "When I do such-and-such I am really myself," it is always a mistake and can eventually lead to soul-destroying trouble. Actually, one is really oneself when one is free of all distraction, both external (noise, other people, phone calls) and internal (the mental buzz, the inner conference, loose and unattached thoughts).

Sometimes people suppose that in order to reach complete reality, to be entirely in the presence of God, one must achieve a total absence of the things which distract us. This is a mistake. Another, rather complicated, factor is at work here. Distraction that we do not recognize as such is still distraction. Distraction that we attempt to reject is still distraction. However, distraction that we both recognize as distraction and accept, without any sort of reservation, is no longer a distraction.

If I am a monk and I stand in church day in and day out feeling resentful, though not quite sure why, then I am being distracted by my feelings. If I am a monk and I stand in the church, day in day out, next to another monk who always sings flat, and I am annoyed by that fact, then I am distracted. However, if I am that monk and I simply accept that the monk is beside me singing flat, that he is not going to stop singing flat, and that his singing is actually every bit as important as my own, then I am no longer distracted. I can enter into the silence even when surrounded by noise.

When we attempt to cut out the distractions that accompany our everyday lives, we often simply replace one distraction with another. Thus, a couple who are not doing too well in their marriage will choose, consciously or not, to have a baby so that they do not have to focus on each other for the next eighteen years. Of course, at the end of the eighteen years, life is considerably different. It may be that the focus of the couple's problems has shifted, and what they considered as problems at the beginning have now quite disappeared, or been replaced by other ones. It is also possible, though, that the couple may meet each other again and find that they still need to do the work—they have just postponed it by eighteen years.

It is not difficult to describe what happens when we distract ourselves, or why. However, when we come beyond our distractions, what happens then? What happens when we are not affected by distraction?

When we cease to be distracted, the heart (or the nous) starts to operate. When the mind is quiet, even for a part of a second, the nous begins the process of recovery. Since its action is subtle rather than obvious, a high degree of inner peace is necessary before we even notice its existence. Setting aside the mind with its intrusive thoughts and the story it writes (which we have called the ego), we find a place unaffected by the constant fragmentation of the mind's efforts. The heart is not affected by fragmentation, although I would think it fair to say that it does miss the mind. The splitting of ourselves into little bits occurs in the mind, not the heart, so when we stop distracting ourselves, we move away from the activity of the mind and the ego and towards the heart. We do not confront ourselves, but rather we *are* ourselves.

When we are completely ourselves, in the present moment, we are in the presence of God—we meet God. Meeting God is not a "doing" activity, but rather a "being" activity. In fact, when we stop all the doing—absolutely *all* the doing—then we begin to be.

When we are completely free from distraction—when there is no "no" left in us—when we are completely focused, then prayer can begin.

Scripture provides us with some powerful images about the nature of prayer. Two examples stand out in particular, one from the Old Testament and one from the New.

And there he [Elijah] went into a cave, and spent the night in that place; and behold, the word of the LORD came to him, and He said to him, "What are you doing here, Elijah?" So he said, "I have been very zealous for the LORD God of hosts; for the children of Israel have forsaken Your covenant, torn down Your altars, and killed Your prophets with the sword. I alone am left; and they seek to take my life." Then He said, "Go out, and stand on the mountain before the LORD." And behold, the LORD passed by, and a great and strong wind tore into the mountains and broke the rocks in pieces before the LORD, but the LORD was not in the wind; and after the wind an earthquake, but the LORD was not in the earthquake; and after the earthquake a fire, but the LORD was not in the fire; and after the fire a still small voice. (1 Kings 19:9–12)

Like Elijah, we generally expect God to be in the earthquakes, the fires, and the wind. However, it is in the "still small voice" (translated elsewhere as "the sound of silence," and in the Septuagint as "the sound of a tiny, gentle breeze") that he actually encounters God.

The New Testament example is also well known:

Now it happened as they went that He entered a certain village; and a certain woman named Martha welcomed Him into her house. And she had a sister called Mary, who also sat at Jesus' feet and heard His word. But Martha was distracted with much serving, and she approached Him and said, "Lord, do You not care that my sister has left me to serve alone? Therefore tell her to help me." And Jesus answered and said to her, "Martha, Martha, you are worried and troubled about many things. But one thing is needed, and Mary has chosen that good part, which will not be taken away from her." (Luke 10:38–42)

This beautiful story, so reticent, yet so revealing of the relationship between Jesus and these two sisters, provides a wonderful word-icon of what discipleship actually means. In any normal situation, we would expect Jesus to respond to Martha's complaints by standing up, encouraging Mary to help her sister, and perhaps even helping her Himself. That is not what happens here.

Martha is full of distraction. The things she is fretting about appear real enough, important enough, to take all her attention. But she is missing the entire point of her life. Jesus is present right there (as He is for us also), but instead of spending time in silence with Him, as her sister Mary is doing, she is concerned with the ephemera, things which in the eternal dimension are insignificant.

Some of us lead entire lives filled with insignificance. We need to take steps to move from insignificance to reality. There are many ways of doing this, but one that has been favored by the Orthodox Church for many centuries is the use of the Jesus Prayer ("Lord Jesus Christ, Son of God, have mercy on me, a sinner").

There are many ways to use the Jesus Prayer that encourage the very sort of attention Jesus says is, in effect, the most important thing in life. Many people use the Jesus Prayer as they go through their day, particularly at times when they are doing routine things that allow them to be mentally disengaged, or on occasions when they are waiting for something to happen (sitting at a red light, waiting for a bus, and so on). They will say the prayer at, or near, conversational speed, and will take care to bring their attention back to the prayer whenever their minds cause them to be distracted.

Another way to use the prayer, however, is to go to a place where there will be no disturbance (here the full force of Jesus' words about locking yourself in your room may be applied), then reciting the prayer very slowly. Some people find it is better to shorten the traditional words of the prayer for this purpose, perhaps only using five words: "Lord Jesus Christ, have mercy."

Here the words are important, as we would expect, but so too is the silence between the words. We say a word, slowly, listening to the sound of the word in our heads (or on our lips), but then we listen carefully to the silence between the words, before going on to the next one. We have no expectations, and indeed, nothing has to happen. We do not expect to think anything, feel anything, or hear anything. We simply listen to the silence.

In the world at large, there is a silence which is simply the lack of all noise. This is a negative silence, a silence waiting to be filled. However, in the spiritual life we discover another, much more valuable sort of silence, and that is the silence which is the voice of God. The two sorts of silence sound similar, but they are not the same. The silence sought by the hesychasts[10] is the voice of God. Within this silence we are bathed in the goodness and love of God.

Silence is the language of God. Everything else is a mistranslation.

~: INTERCESSION :~

There is one area in which distraction can be used to good effect, although in a deeply spiritualized fashion. While news, conversations, and gossip form a lively part of the distracted human existence, these are all areas that can be transformed by the practice of intercession.

Intercession is praying for people and situations. Typically, in the Orthodox Church, we do not pray for specific outcomes, but simply make the act of remembering someone or something before God in prayer a gesture of love. "Lord, remember . . ." followed by a name or a situation is quite sufficient. Again, we do not rely on mental images here, nor are our emotions of any particular significance.

Particularly powerful are the prayers we offer for those who have wronged us or hurt us in some way. Sometimes it is good to make a list of such people (one hopes it will not be too long), and to undertake to pray for those people in particular at a regular time each day.

---

10 The word *hesychast* comes from the Greek word *hesychia*, which means "silence." It is generally applied to a movement among Orthodox monastics and others whose way of life is motivated by the *Philokalia*. Hesychasm might be described as the mystical framework of modern Orthodox faith and practice.

This is a potent way of encouraging our emotions to change after we have met the first mandatory requirement of forgiving such people.

Our care and concerns for other people, for our country, for our planet, are not all empty, nor are they all selfish or egotistical. This is demonstrated in the very powerful experience of bringing concerns to God in prayer. This is not the intercession that starts out by pointing out what mistakes God is making in the running of the world, followed by a list of things we would like Him to do about it. That practice is simply another aspect of the ego's desire to control, an empty soul-less activity which leads us further away from God, even while we think that because we are participating in something "religious" we must be progressing in the other direction.

Intercession is not a matter of telling God what to do, even with the best of possible intentions. Nor is it a question of trying to change God's mind about something. Intercession is simply a matter of bringing the concerns of our own lives—friends, relatives, but also enemies and competitors—to the throne of God and leaving them there. Any person and any subject can be brought to God.

When someone bothers us, bringing that person to God in prayer is very powerful, but the effect of the prayerful action is more likely to be seen in oneself than in the other person. If we feel dislike for a person, or other stronger emotions, there is nothing more powerful than bringing that person to God in prayer. This we can do until the feelings subside, since there is nothing God cannot tame and enliven—even our own personal dislikes and prejudices.

Like an offering of fruit, of grain or wine or oil, we bring things to God, not that He lacks them in any sense, but simply because He accepts our offerings. Intercessions are like that. We simply offer our concerns to God. We do not pray for specific outcomes, and we do not demand particular results, since to do so would place our own desires as the point of the prayer, whereas in reality the sole and entire aim of prayer is to discover the will of God. It may seem rather obvious to state that we do not discover the will of God by simply repeating our own demands over and over again.

Nor do we expect to leave off our prayer with a sense of certainty as to what the will of God is—at least, not most of the time. In most cases, we are no clearer in our minds after prayer than we were before. The clarity, where and when it exists, exists in the root of our being, in the deep recesses of who we are. We rarely pay attention to that extent, since it requires effort (as opposed to listening to the constant chatter of our minds) and courage to find the still and silent center of our being, the wordless expression of our contact with God. That place is, of course, the nous, the heart.

When we encounter God, we have to be prepared to meet someone who exists, who functions and acts in ways quite unlike anything we may expect. So strong is our tendency to try to make God act in a way we might expect that there is a special word for it: anthropomorphism.

In the realm of love, in particular, we have much to learn. The love of God is something completely beyond our experience in the human world. For us, love is a choice—accompanied by feelings, often strong feelings, which cause us to pick a partner, a soul-mate, or a friend. It also means that we reject others in these roles. In this respect, our love is limited—we love this person, but not that one. We only have enough love for a small number of people; there is not enough to go round.

The love of God is so completely at the other end of the spectrum that it sometimes might appear to be something else entirely. The love of God is not limited, since in God it is impossible for there to be love for one person but not for another. In fact, lack of love for anyone would mean that it is not love at all. When we say things like, "I love all my children/parishioners/students equally," we usually mean we do not love any of them very much. Yet God's love ceases to be love at all if it is measured in any sense.

The love of God is not earned—there is nothing we could possibly do to earn it. It is simply the natural state of God's Being. When we reflect His love (as the moon reflects the light of the sun, or the smile of a child reflects the smile of his mother or father), we are also in that natural state. In that moment, we are operating from the heart. Fear and suspicion have no place here; they only exist properly in the mind of mankind.

The Orthodox liturgy is careful to engage our senses—all five of the physical senses, and perhaps others as well. The icons, the music, the incense—these are not simply *aides memoires*, reminders; they are pointers towards the present moment, the "acceptable time,"[11] the moment of reality in which the liturgy lives. If we allow ourselves to be distracted by anything, to let our minds drift and wander, sometimes very far away from where we are, it is both sensible and useful to go back to our primary senses to bring ourselves back into focus and harmony with what is going on around us.

Sometimes we go to church and there is nothing but distraction: the chanter sings too loudly or off-key, the celebrant's actions are awkward, the sermon is too long, or the liturgy is interrupted unnecessarily. All these things, and much worse, can happen, since the treasure of the Divine Liturgy is delivered into the hands of mere mortals. In some ways, this might be the greatest weakness of the liturgy, but it is also its greatest teaching point, since it encourages mankind to experience heaven.

At the end of St. Basil's Liturgy, the one preferred by the Church for its most precious moments, the priest says a prayer right before the dismissal of the people: "We have accomplished the liturgy, as far as we are able to do so." This is our commitment to God, the promise of the liturgy, that it will take our awareness, our knowledge, our artistry, and our hope to the highest level, to the very limits of our ability. This is, of course, true at any liturgy, not just that of St. Basil.

Our ability to concentrate is actually quite poor. Even with all the help afforded by the physical setting of the liturgy, we can find ourselves quite distanced from what is going on. We find it very difficult to switch our minds off. It is difficult, but not impossible. It is something we do not learn to do in the normal course of events. On the contrary, our training in schools and colleges is generally to keep

---

11 This is a way of conveying the notion of "now" seen not as one instance of the present moment among many others, but rather as the awareness of eternity in time. See 2 Corinthians 6:2.

our minds active. However, in prayer we do not need to think—we need to be.

The liturgy explicitly invites us to do this at one of its high points. At the Great Entrance, we sing what is probably the most ancient hymn in our liturgy—a one-word hymn that comes to us straight from our Jewish prehistory: Alleluia. The hymn is preceded by the instructions required to sing this one-word hymn correctly: "Let us, who represent the cherubim in a mystical way, and sing the thrice-holy hymn to the life-giving Trinity, now lay aside all the cares of this life, so that we may receive the King of all, invisibly surrounded by the hosts of angels: Alleluia." Laying aside the cares of this life is essential if we are to fulfill our role as human auxiliaries to the angelic forces. Yet, it is precisely the cares of this life that are conjured up and given life in our minds. Notice, too, that the hymn insists on the present moment as being that when the action takes place. In this beautiful example of Byzantine clarity, we see how "now" and "the cares of this life" cannot exist together. Here cause and effect flow into each other—the awareness of "now" excludes the "cares of this life."

❧ THE DIVINE LITURGY AND LANGUAGE ☙

A number of factors can make our participation in the liturgy something of a challenge. For example, we use a variety of languages in our tradition. The Orthodox Church throughout the world has a relationship with language that many will find strange. Certainly, Greek Orthodox tend to use Greek, Russian Orthodox tend to use Russian (or at least a historical form related to Russian) in their services. A Greek parish may use Greek in its services even though the vast majority of the congregation does not speak Greek on a daily basis. Even if the people do speak Greek, the language used in church is far removed from the language of Greek households.

In fact, very few people might have anything more than a vague notion of what the words are saying at any given moment. The words might form familiar sounds, and it is possible that a number of people present know the sounds quite well, but only have a vague notion of what the words actually mean. Sometimes, in the most traditional parishes, there will be groups of fairly elderly well-meaning ladies joining in with all the parts of the liturgy: the choir's part and even the priest's part. There is no guarantee, however, that they know what the individual words mean, even though they probably have a good sense of what they mean all together.

In these languages the congregation celebrates the services throughout the year, and the services are full of poetic references. On a major feast day, the main theme of the feast will be presented in hundreds of different ways; it will be compared with other major events in the life of the Church, it will be rolled around in thought and hymn, floated upon a sea of biblical imagery and theological contemplation. It enters and re-enters the imagination of the worshipper, sometimes with great subtlety, at other times in an exultant, almost triumphant manner. Each major feast day has its own "buzzwords," its own vocabulary, available to those who listen even when they do not understand every reference. Keywords from the main theme of the day, such as "the Holy of Holies" on the feast of the Entry of the Mother of God into the Temple, "the Jordan" and "the Baptist" on Epiphany, help us to keep focused, keep present.

For most Orthodox, during most of the history of the Church, the language used in the services has been a little obscure at best, a completely foreign language at worst. Naturally, every word was originally written to convey a meaning—to mean something to the people who were listening. Gradually, though, this literal understanding was replaced with a more general acquaintance—where certain words were readily understood (often the most important, and the most repeated), while the rest of the service, for all its subtlety and elevated language, became a blur in the mind of the worshipper. This is certainly true for the services of Vespers and Matins, served in our churches in an abbreviated version, and more often than not left to monks and nuns to celebrate them in their fullness. For the average lay person, they become a blur of theology, a faint hum of half-understood images. Sometimes there is a familiarity with the sounds, with little or no corresponding understanding.

Contrary to what some people would like to believe, most Orthodox Christians of most nationalities throughout most of recent history have not had a clear understanding of most of the words they hear in church. The major exception to this situation is the Church of Romania, where all the services are now served in a language the people understand. The Church of Finland and the Church in Japan have followed similar paths. We can also add to this number all those churches founded by immigrants throughout the world where the language of the new country has been adopted.

This factor has a positive as well as a negative aspect. Worship is not essentially an intellectual process—not a thinking exercise: it is an activity. Sometimes people who are new to the Church want to follow the services with a book. There are several problems here. First, there is no book, even for the Divine Liturgy, which is easy to follow. Depending on the day, there always seem to be reasons why the service goes as it does and not as the book states it ought to.

Secondly, simply reading along as the priest, the choir, and the chanters and readers do their parts is really not what is required. Much better is to stand still with your eyes open, watching and listening, and (in whatever way you feel suitable) participating in the service. We do not go to church to understand. Rather, we go to church to meet God, and there is probably a great deal of that meeting which will have nothing to do with understanding.

If a language is being used that you understand, you can take advantage of the situation in a number of ways. Stay as present as possible, gently bringing yourself back to the present moment whenever your mind starts to wander away. Pick out the main themes in what is being sung or chanted and allow the kaleidoscope of images to surround you. Punctuate particular expressions with a sign of the cross, the function of which is always to bring you back to the present if you have wandered, or to deepen and reinforce your presence if you have not.

If the language being used is difficult to understand, you are completely free to concentrate on your presence, and this can be achieved by concentrating on staying in your body. During prayer in the Orthodox tradition, we are encouraged to go deeper and deeper into our bodies, to be physically more and more present. The sign of the cross and prostrations are elements of this tradition. We are actually they have no physical bodies such as ours to help them.

If the language used is not what you prefer and you have no power
to change that, the only authentic thing to do is to accept the fact.
That may have some hidden benefit also, as we saw earlier in this
chapter. Once a distraction is accepted completely, it ceases to be
a distraction. In other words, once you have accepted the language
being used, with all its benefits and drawbacks, then you can go back
to being in the presence of God. So long as you listen to your mind
complaining, you might as well be at Safeway or the public library.
The minute you can accept everything, you are free to be in the presence of God once more.

❧ POINTS TO WATCH ☙

One of the most important things we need to watch when we are in
church is that our time there is not wasted or squandered. The church
is not a place to give your mind an exercise. The mind specializes in
being in any time but the present, and anywhere but here. Since the
time in church should be a concentrated effort to experience the present moment, the mind is not actually very useful.

There are several ways in which the mind can be engaged, and to
know this before it happens can help us to maintain our concentra-
tion. Our aim is to be like the candles burning in front of the icons:
simply to be who we are for the duration of time we are there.

One area the mind loves to get into is being judgmental. One of the
specific commandments of Jesus is that we should not be judgmental
of each other, and yet we spend an inordinate amount of time making
judgments about people and things and events. These judgments are
normally completely useless and unnecessary.

What is required in the liturgy is the ability to "be" without the
need to judge. Love, in its broadest sense, cannot be based on judgment, because that would imply that we have a choice as to whether
we love or not. Love is, according to Jesus, a moral imperative, one of
His most obvious commandments. In the liturgy this is presented in
a very particular form: "Let us love one another, that with oneness of

mind we may confess: the Father, the Son, and the Holy Spirit, the Trinity, one in essence and undivided." It is worthy of note that the "oneness of mind" in this sentence actually translates the Greek "oneness of nous."

It is a great deal easier to be nonjudgmental about people we do not know than about people we do know. When we are standing in church, thoughts and feelings about the people who are standing or sitting nearby are almost unavoidable. "I wish that person would stop singing," "I hope that woman stops her child crying," "The choir is doing a dreadful job today," and so on.

One of the most dangerous traps of spiritual behavior is to make a judgment about someone with a view to "praying" for them. Making oneself feel superior about someone else is a very poor way to start praying for him or her. I used to attend a group that met at my aunt's house twice a month. It was officially an intercession group. However, since each of the persons being prayed for was discussed in great detail, including bringing the other members of the group up to date with what was happening, the prayer session quickly degenerated into a sort of spiritually licit gossip session.

If, when you are standing in church, a thought or a feeling about someone else arises, gently push it aside. There is absolutely no point in getting angry with yourself, or even disappointed, since that simply sets up a struggle inside yourself that reinforces the effect of taking you away from where you want to be. Having pushed the thought aside, you can resume your place in the body of Christ, and like the angels, stand around the throne in silent adoration.

Another area where we can easily make a mistake is to refuse to accept the reality of what is going on around us. Here, the Serenity Prayer, so beloved of Twelve Step fellowships, provides a pointer: "God grant me the serenity to accept the things I cannot change, courage to change the things I can, and wisdom to know the difference." The wisdom to know the difference is, of course, the most important factor here, since a difference definitely exists between the things we would like to change and the things we can change. The difference between these two categories is crucial to our understanding, since in any given situation, whatever cannot be changed needs to be accepted.

It may be appropriate to consider something explicitly spiritual at this point. The Orthodox Church has a profound awareness of the significance of the Cross, but this experience has never focused primarily on the pain suffered by Jesus. When we look at Jesus on the Cross, we see not so much a man in great pain, but something much more miraculous. There, on the Cross, we see Jesus in complete acceptance of the will of God. It is His surrender, total, focused, and voluntary, that elevated the terrible and life-destroying action of humanity into a divine moment of supreme victory for life and love and joy and peace. There is much about Jesus that would be impossible for us to emulate. However, His sense of presence is something we can at the very least attempt, particularly when we are standing in church. That presence is fueled by acceptance and ignited by complete surrender.

Every action in church should be taken with care. This is certainly true of those ministering at the altar, but is no less true of those in the congregation. Careless movement or anything that hints at lack of complete presence is to be avoided. On the other hand, there should not be a hint of showmanship or ostentatious movement either. Everything should reflect a great naturalness and great care. Every moment should be treasured as if there were no other, which indeed turns out to be the case. Casual attitudes should be avoided, since we are in the presence of the King of the universe. On the other hand, we should deal kindly with those around us, avoiding any movement or expression that could be regarded as judgmental, since tight-lipped, mean-minded religious practice is a very ugly thing.

It takes a great deal of effort to be able to remain present in the presence of God. This means that for most people the effort looks too demanding. There does not appear to be any payoff. Yet, at another level, this is the destination of the human being, the high point of existence. The odd thing is that it is not what we necessarily expect. We may assume, at least, that the experience is likely to be one highly charged with emotion. Such is not the case. In fact, the experience is rather beyond emotion, a place where emotion cannot reach. Emotion may take us there, but it cannot be at our arrival, nor can it be relied upon. The same is true of thought, whether on a level of thinking in general, of understanding, or of the application of intelligence or rationality in particular. These things can lead us to the moment of encounter, but they cannot make the encounter.

The important thing to remember here is that if we are full of emotion or satisfied that we have approached God through the power of our own thought, not only are we not at the goal, but we may not even be on the right path. As already stated, the goal is a state called *nepsis* by the Fathers of the Church. It is a place of intense awareness, and it is accompanied by an almost complete lack of thought and emotion. There is even a lack of what one might call re-thinking (just as there is reaction to an action). The experience is achieved in great stillness.

~: BIBLE READING :~

At the center of the Divine Liturgy is Scripture—not in a dead and distant way, but as a living expression of the presence of God. It is the task of the members of the Body of Christ to bring the word of Scripture into the "eternal now" by their attentiveness. In the Divine Liturgy, Scripture is actually in its own environment, since it is within the liturgy that its words find their true context. Strictly speaking, there is no such thing as "Bible study" in the Orthodox Church. That would simply involve applying the mind to the words of Scripture, attempting to get some meaning out of them. In contrast, when we encounter Scripture in the liturgy, it is from a place of complete presence. The process is much more "Bible listening" than "Bible study."

Although it may be inappropriate to talk of studying the Bible, it is by no means inappropriate to champion the cause of Bible reading. Orthodox Christians need to know the Bible very thoroughly, since all the services are based on themes that come from biblical sources. Moreover, the services themselves come from a culture in which knowledge of the sacred texts must have been common.

Hearing Scripture rightly belongs in the context of the liturgy. However, the way the readings are divided makes this difficult, unless one is fortunate enough to be able to go to church every day of the year. Listening, even with great care, to the readings on Sunday mornings means hearing less than one-seventh of all that is read in

Scriptures on the major feast days of the Church.

Reading the whole of the Bible in a year is not an impossible task, requiring only about ten or fifteen minutes per day. There are even special "One Year" Bibles in a variety of translations which divide the readings into manageable sections. These, when read from a place of great silence, provide more than enough nourishment for spiritual development. The words of Scripture also open up the entire body of patristic writing, the distinctively Orthodox commentary on meeting God.

The best of all possible worlds is to read the Bible in some systematic way, as suggested, but also to read the particular sections of scripture associated with church services on a particular day, as outlined on an Orthodox Church calendar. Combining one set of readings with morning prayer and the other with prayers at night may be a solution.

A few details need to be kept fresh in one's awareness in order to avoid some of the more obvious mental traps sometimes encountered when reading from Scripture. When reading, it is necessary, consciously or unconsciously, to find meaning in what is being read, and it is the mind which provides that information. Every word, both as a separate unit and within the context of the sentence in which it is written, has to be interpreted by the reader's mind. There is no such thing as a "literal" meaning of any sentence, since the whole point of writing is that thoughts and ideas be communicated through words. The thoughts and feelings of the writer are made available to the thoughts and feelings of the reader, in order that communication can occur as a sort of resonance between the experience of the writer and that of the reader.

By necessity, reading starts as a mental experience. When we hear a word or see it written down, the brain goes into a flurry of activity. At great speed, it compares that word, or the sound of that word, with every other occasion on which it may have been encountered, whether in a written or a spoken context. The next stage is to compare the context of the written word—where it stands in the sentence, the chapter, the book—with memories of similar usage elsewhere.

Even though human beings may react to certain words in a seemingly similar manner, there is actually no guarantee that we all understand a given word in exactly the same way under all or any circumstances. For example, the word "banana" will mean very different things to people who like bananas (nourishment, a pleasant taste, nostalgic memories of eating bananas, beautiful memories of people associated with bananas), people who do not like bananas (nausea, images of rotting fruit, memories of slipping on a banana skin), and people who have never seen a banana (confused images that try to make sense of the data available).

If unanimity of understanding is difficult to achieve with the word "banana," it is all the more difficult with a word that represents something intangible. For example, the words "freedom" and "beauty" can mean almost anything, depending not only on the experience, but also the intention, of the person who uses them. Unless another person knows both the experience and the intention of the speaker, it is almost impossible to be sure that the listener understands what the first person is saying.

The most reliable way of understanding a particular word is, as nearly as possible, to enter into the situation or worldview of the person who used it. To give a simple example, St. Paul tells us that all Scripture is given to us for our edification (2 Timothy 3:16). Here it is important to know what we mean by the word "Scripture," but much more important to know what St. Paul meant by the word. Otherwise, we are likely to misunderstand what he is saying. We might assume that St. Paul is referring to the Bible as we know it, including his own works. This is not historically possible. The Gospels were not yet written down in their present form when St. Paul was writing, and there is nothing to suggest that Paul considered his own letters to be Scripture. Any examination of the mind of St. Paul when he wrote that word would be likely to reveal that he is referring solely to the Scriptures contained in what we call the Old Testament, and even then we cannot be absolutely sure what he meant, since there was no standardized book of the Old Testament at the time. To think otherwise is to hijack the words of St. Paul and use them for our own purposes, based on our own presuppositions.

Many groups of people use the Holy Scriptures that make up the Bible. For Jews, the words of the Old Testament, and particularly the first five books of the Bible, sometimes known as the Torah (Genesis, Exodus, Leviticus, Numbers, and Deuteronomy), enshrine everything that is special in the way Jews think about God. For Christians, the words of the Old Testament are also sacred; they are treated with a great deal of respect, since they show the development of the whole story of the relationship between God and His people up to the period before the birth of Jesus.

However, just as the words of the Torah are especially sacred to Jewish people, so the words of the four Gospels, Matthew, Mark, Luke, and John, are especially sacred to Orthodox Christians—and of those words, the ones spoken by Jesus Himself are the most treasured. The rest of the Bible is sacred, certainly, and very important, but it is in the words of the Gospel that the Orthodox Church finds her fullest expression.

The Orthodox Church stands quite apart from those groups, both Christian and non-Christian, that treat all the words of Scripture equally, taking a verse from here and comparing it with a verse from there, attempting to make sense of the Word of God as if it were a difficult jigsaw puzzle. The Book of the Four Gospels—and within their pages the words of Christ Himself, whose teaching is for all time the supreme guide of the Orthodox Church—stands at the center of all Orthodox experience.

For this reason, it is the Book of the Gospels that lies on the holy table in the altar. It is the Book of the Gospels that is placed, open, in the middle of major church councils. This is not merely a symbolic presence: Christ Himself speaks through the words of the Gospels. The open Book of the Gospels is placed on the head of the person being ordained bishop, and it is also held above those who are being anointed with oil in the service for the sick.

The honor paid to the Book of the Gospels is no empty gesture. It is simply the way in which the Church responds to the sound of her most precious possession. However, the words need to be spoken in order to be heard.

~: CHAPTER 4 :~

Askesis—
Making the Sanctified Effort

*W*HEN CONSIDERING THE TITLE FOR THE PRESENT book, I intended *Bread & Water, Wine & Oil* to refer to the material elements employed in the various Mysteries of the Church. However, I was somewhat concerned that if people shortened the title conversationally to "Bread & Water," that might give the wrong impression.

The phrase "bread and water" leaps out from my childhood memories of stories about people being thrown in prison, about pirates making people walk the plank, and kings and queens chopping people's heads off. French aristocrats were thrown out of their palaces during the Revolution, and if they were lucky enough to miss the ministrations of Madame Guillotine, they eked out a saddened and desperate existence in a windowless prison cell, being fed bread and water twice a week, if the prison guard happened to remember.

The reality is that, if a person is hungry and thirsty enough, bread and water provide the most delicious, nutritious, and satisfying sustenance. However, very few people in my world are ever hungry or thirsty enough for this to happen. In affluent parts of the world, hunger and thirst are almost unknown. We fear being hungry and thirsty as if these states were harbingers of death, or at least of extreme discomfort. Therefore we eat long before hunger starts, and drink long before thirst.

As with pains of all descriptions, we tend to try to push hunger away. However, at some point along the spiritual path we learn that pain is a teacher, and we actually derive benefit from accepting it rather than rejecting it. Far from being an enemy, hunger has been given to us in order to teach us the finer things in life.

~: WHY DO WE FAST? :~

The Greek word *askesis* (from which we get the English word "ascetic") means "exercise." It generally refers to the practice of prayer, fasting, making prostrations, and in other ways modifying our behavior to bring it in line with the spiritual life.

Askesis is not, and cannot be, an attempt to please God with our pain, or even with our effort. If we do that, we reduce God to the role of manipulative overseer. We always have to guard against projecting onto God human characteristics that belong not to Him, but to us.

Askesis is rather a matter of exercise, in the manner that an athlete exercises in order to prepare for a race. The athlete does not, in the end, resent his hard work, because he knows he is doing it for a good reason. We are all "in training" spiritually, and the rhythm of the feasts and fasts of the Orthodox Church allows us to intersperse rigorous periods of training with other times that are more relaxed. Lent and Holy Week together constitute the training period *par excellence* of the Church, with its own unique qualities and opportunities. This period is preceded and followed by weeks when we do not fast at all. However, the opposite of fasting is never self-indulgence, and feasting certainly need never be an occasion of decadence.

But there are other dimensions of askesis, equally important to the element of training. In nature, we can observe that God's actions are almost always marked by a sense of restraint, and this is what we should seek to emulate. God has a gentleness we rarely find in our own lives. His actions are to do with subtle balances: just enough light, just enough darkness; just enough oxygen, just enough carbon dioxide; just enough acid, just enough alkali; just enough regularity to make life somewhat predictable (sunsets, tides), just enough surprises to make life unpredictable (earthquakes, floods). In this way, God makes a unique environment in which each one of us is ideally capable of making the spiritual progress each of us is called to make.

Fasting is like that balance God puts into creation. Restraint and fasting characterize the lives of those who enjoy life to its fullest. How can someone be really contented who has not known hunger? How can someone really experience the joy of Pascha without having fasted during the weeks of Lent?

Fasting is not, and never can be, a punishment. Rather, it is a therapeutic tool by which we are brought closer to where we need to be, both physically and spiritually. Nor is fasting a matter of self-control or self-discipline. These elements turn spiritual fasting into something ugly—as if some sort of grim determination would make us more pleasing to God.

Nor is fasting a matter of demonstrating to the world that pain and hardship can be borne. Those who refuse to wash their faces or brush their teeth and thus surreptitiously let the world know they are fasting are no better than the people Christ condemns. Fasting, of itself, brings no particular merit. Many are those who fast rigorously, but make everyone around them suffer. That, strictly speaking, is not fasting either, but some sort of self-deception.

The purpose of fasting from midnight before Holy Communion is to heighten our awareness so that from the moment we awaken, the desire to be united with our Lord in Holy Communion should be the uppermost theme in our lives. Nothing is more important than that, including food.

There is another element of fasting that has been growing in people's awareness in the last few years. As guardians of God's creation, we have fallen down on the job. We have done great damage to our planet and are in danger of doing greater harm in the future unless we change our ways. We have done the damage by being unaware, listening to the demands of our minds, not the desires of our hearts. We have taken more than we need. We have not used resources in moderation. Fasting teaches us that we can actually live happy, fulfilled lives using very few resources. Far from bringing us happiness, the desire to have and own more and more brings us to our own destruction.

Fasting is important in teaching us the value of relying on God. The basic fault in man might be expressed as his desire to take the place of God and set himself up in his own world as the one controlling factor. This goal is neither salutary nor possible. Fasting helps us to regain the essential awareness that we are creatures in God's world, that we are a part of, not superior to, the rest of creation, and that ultimately, there is only place for one God, and that place has already been taken.

Each one of us in this fallen world has a sense of self (the ego) which is driven by the human mind and the logismoi it contains. In each case, this ego tries to take the place of God to a greater or lesser extent. The spiritual path encourages us to heal precisely in this area. In this respect, the work of salvation is going on all the time, restoring God to His rightful place in the life of each individual. This is "the coming of the Kingdom." Fasting is not the only contributing factor in this process, but it is an important one.

~: HOW DO WE FAST? :~

Obviously, it is not easy to fast well, and most people need a little practice. Good fasting depends, more than anything else, on a good attitude. There can be nothing ego-building in one's desire to fast; to fast for the wrong reasons is as bad as not fasting at all.

The Orthodox Church makes fasting easier by stipulating when and how it happens. If we were to choose our own fast days, a certain amount of pride would be bound to slip in, and pride is the one element that cannot be present if we are to fast well. The Church calendar lets us know whether it is a fast day or not, and with that information we are then free to decide whether or not to comply.

In a monastery or a well-regulated household, this is easy enough: the correct food in the correct amounts is mysteriously provided for us at the correct time. I have to say, that sort of fasting strikes me as something of a luxury. For those of us who have to drive around towns filled with McDonald's, Burger Kings, or even wonderful vegetarian restaurants, for those who have to do the cooking and for those who have to cope with the eating habits of other family members, colleagues, or parishioners, fasting is more complicated.

However, each one of us is in a unique position, and in that unique position it is possible, perhaps with some good spiritual advice, to come up with a plan of action that will satisfy our own spiritual needs as well as pleasing the people with whom we live or work. There are situations in which fasting is not a matter of changing eating habits at all, but of adapting some other form of behavior instead. For this to happen well, it is good to consult with someone else.

We have to be on our guard against thinking that fasting has any virtue in itself. Not eating meat on Wednesday or Friday is not a virtue *per se*, and certainly the minute we condemn another person for eating meat on those days, we lose that very important balance fasting is supposed to bring in the first place.

Jesus asks us to be very careful when we fast. It has to be a secret activity, although sometimes, as in a monastery, it can be something of an open secret. Thus, it is something we do not talk about, because the moment we do we are so prone to start boasting or judging that we are likely to inject the fasting with one of those darker human qualities we are trying to avoid.

This means, too, that we have to fast without any ostentation. Going to a fine restaurant, then explaining to the waiter that we are fasting and thus require special care and attention of a self-serving kind ("what exactly was the onion fried in before it was put in the ratatouille, because I cannot eat anything fried in animal fat, because I am fasting") is obviously not a good thing to do. To go to the restaurant and quietly pick out the things from the menu that it may be suitable to eat, then to take what you are given, would be a much better solution. Although sometimes unavoidable, visits to restaurants should perhaps be better left to nonfasting periods in the first place. Fasting is something best done at home, and learning to prepare fasting foods for oneself is a good part of the overall exercise.

Sometimes fasting turns people into grim, closed-hearted types who begrudge everything to everyone and really think their misery is pleasing to God. I think they are mistaken. If our outer attitudes are anything less than serene, cheerful, and loving, there is something very wrong with the way we are fasting.

A rather surprising element in fasting was pointed out to me by a monk in whose monastery it was the custom to eat nothing but bread and water on Fridays. When we were talking about this, I made some comment in my naïveté that it must make the regular food on Saturday taste much better. The monk looked at me with one of those monastic glances that are so eloquent—not quite pity, not quite not. "At the beginning," he said, "that was true. Gradually you learn to enjoy the bread and water for its own sake."

Lastly, fasting is not something about which to be too fastidious. It is a largely symbolic activity, and the edges are a bit fuzzy. There is room for give and take, and legalism is hardly appropriate. To feast sumptuously on caviar, shrimp, and lobster and wash it down with a fine whiskey, while perfectly "legal," is hardly in accordance with the spirit of the exercise.

And if you are going to say something nasty about someone on Great and Holy Friday, you might as well be chewing on a pork chop at the same time.

~: THE PHYSICAL DIMENSION OF PRAYER :~

Another distinctive feature of Orthodox life is "physical" prayer. This too is part of the ascetic life.

In the writings of the saints of the Church, we are often reminded that prayer actually involves our bodies in many ways. In the West, there is a tendency to regard prayer as a mental exercise, to use imagination and thought, to attempt to reach God using mental powers. In the Orthodox tradition this is not so. The Fathers recognize the inability of the human mind to help much in this process, given its fallen state and its divorce from the heart. For Orthodox, prayer is actually a matter of going deeper and deeper into the body, not of trying to escape from it.

The human body is not an optional extra in the spiritual process, nor is it a necessary evil. As a Church, we look forward to resurrection, not just to immortality. The body is going with us as we get closer and closer to God, even though it is bound to undergo transformation, sometimes drastic transformation, along the path. It is no accident, then, that our bodies take part in the Holy Mysteries, since they are intimately involved with our salvation.

For these reasons, physical prayer becomes more and more important as we grow in awareness of our relationship with God.

One of my first impressions of Orthodox worship was during a Vespers of Forgiveness service, the night before the beginning of Great Lent. Here each worshipper approaches the priest, and then the priest and the worshipper prostrate towards each other, asking forgiveness. The first person then stands to one side, and the next prostrates with the priest, then with the first person, before adding himself to the receiving line. By the time the ceremony is over, each member of the congregation has prostrated towards the priest and every other member of the congregation, asking forgiveness. This is a deeply moving ceremony.

The act of prostration (*metanoia*, the same word Greek uses for "repentance") in prayer is an extremely important one, and one we need to rediscover. It reminds us of the importance of the human body in prayer. The body participates as much in our path to God (which is not particularly obvious) as it does in any sin we may commit along the way (which is sometimes very obvious indeed—it is difficult to gossip if you have no tongue).

Whether we make a prostration once or many times is not important. The person who can make one prostration, even very slowly with the help of a chair, makes a statement about him or herself and about God that is worth thousands of pages of explanation.

A prostration in prayer is a visual icon of the entire Christian experience. It is a reminder of the Mystery of Holy Baptism, because we die in Christ, then rise again with Him in each prostration. It puts us in touch with the ground and reminds us of our identity with the physical world, an identity urban life does a great deal to diminish or abolish altogether. Finally, it is a gesture of acknowledgement of the absolute sovereignty of God and a reminder that the only authentic prayer is "Thy will be done."

The spiritual world values the one who knows how to prostrate more than anyone who receives adulation from others. The heroes of the spiritual life tend to be little-known men and women living secret lives of prayer, prostrating themselves humbly to the Master of the Universe, rather than statesmen, leaders of armies, or indeed anyone else that the world describes as "great."

In some of the ascetic literature of the Orthodox tradition, of which there is a great deal, one is sometimes given the impression that askesis is all to do with struggle. Prostrations become no more than "teaching the body a jolly good lesson," trying to subdue its not-very-spiritual demands. Fasting teaches the body to moderate its desires, and so on.

This may present an appealing image to some, but we as Westerners have to be on our guard against developing a body-hating spirituality in which the force of our ego struggles to rule supreme. This is very far from where we need to be. There is no place for self-condemnation, whipping ourselves, or damaging our bodies.

There is a struggle, but it is not conducted by forcing one's will upon one's own body (or anyone or anything else). The struggle consists of accepting the will of God and allowing God to accomplish the transformation so needed in our lives.

The great ascetics know that they have nothing to boast about. Indeed, their only authentic response to God is gratitude.

~: CHAPTER 5 :~

The Sanctification of Time

A MAN WAS SENT TO PRISON FOR SEVENTY YEARS. HE spent his days standing on tiptoe, trying to look out the window of his cell, through which he could just catch a glimpse of the sky.

Looking at the sky, he thought about what it would be like to be free. In his imagination he used to go on long journeys. Sometimes he went into the future and thought about what life would be like after he had finished his time in jail. Some of these thoughts were pleasant. After all, freedom looks wonderful to anyone who does not have it. But sometimes his imagination would take him to places that terrified him. Life in prison certainly has its drawbacks, but at least you do not have to worry about feeding yourself or how to organize your day.

Looking into the future, the prisoner was obsessed with "what ifs." He worried about growing old and being lonely, about getting sick and having no one to care for him, about being scorned or rejected. Often he feared he might not get all the benefits of life that so many other people seemed to have. Feelings of failure, fears of not living up to his potential—whether in his own eyes or in the eyes of people whose approval mattered—formed a major part of his outlook.

Looking into the past was not much more promising. There the predominant thought tended to be "if only"—if only he had not pursued the course of action that had led to his imprisonment. He experienced a certain amount of nostalgia, which gave him feelings of warmth and happiness, but most of the time he felt only regret.

Thus, he spent his days dreaming and remembering, fantasizing and worrying. He felt alienated when he was with others, and completely alone when he was not.

It happened that the day the man was due to leave prison, he had a heart attack and died. In due course, he arrived at the throne of God.

"Where were you when I needed you?" he demanded of God.

"I longed to see you," replied God, "but every day when I came to visit you in your cell, you were not there."

∾ THE MYSTERY OF THE PRESENT MOMENT ∾

We can only meet God in the present moment. This is an area where God chooses to place limits on His own power. We choose whether or not to live in the present moment. Because we can encounter God only in that present moment, whenever we live in the past or in the future, we place ourselves beyond His reach.

We can only make decisions in the present moment. We can only enjoy sights and sounds in the present moment. We can only love or hate in the present moment. The present moment is the interface between ourselves and the rest of the universe, and, more importantly, it is the only point of contact between the individual and God. Of all the possible points of time, only the present moment is available for repentance. The past cannot be taken back and remade. The future remains forever outside our reach.

The present moment may appear to be tiny in duration—so much so that the human mind thinks it hardly exists at all—but in depth it is infinite. Actually, it has no shape or form. There is nothing to measure here, and that really infuriates the mind, since measurement is what the mind is good at. It is remarkable that this quality, so essential to our existence, has no shape. It just is. And it just is in a way the past and future cannot be. The past is a done deal; the future is all guesswork. The formless present moment may be experienced as large or small. In some senses it is of almost no duration. In other ways, it is eternal life. Whichever we choose, it is nevertheless the only space within which we can operate. Indeed, this is the unique means through which we can confront the reality God gives us second by second.

It is odd that we do not consciously spend more time in the present moment than we do.

Unfortunately, the mind blocks the availability of the present moment whenever it has the chance to do so. The mind cannot trust the present moment, since it cannot control it, and is thus almost always at enmity with it. I think this may be part of what Jesus means when He contrasts "this world" with the Kingdom.

The mind cannot control the present moment, the time during which things can arise, so it pretends that it does not exist. This causes a person to behave in a completely unconscious way, forcing the individual to wait for the mind to absorb an event (which by then has become an event in the past) before she or he is allowed to experience it.

One of the important functions of prayer is to bring us into, and to assist us to remain in, the present. It is a vital part of prayer to make sure that we are aiming ourselves at this formless moment. If we wander into the past or the future during that time, we can no longer meet God, and all that we see, hear, and experience is merely the workings of our own imagination.

~: THE SANCTIFICATION OF TIME :~

Participation in the Holy Mysteries places God in our time and gives us a powerful incentive to meet with Him. He provides the *kairos*—"the opportune time" in which we can meet. All we have to do is turn up, preferably with hands clean and faces washed. The kairos can only take place in the present moment. Any present moment will do—each is potentially as miraculous as any other.

Sacramental time, the time of the Mysteries, occurs when eternity breaks in on our world. This brings with it a new set of circumstances not generally experienced in everyday life. In the presence of God, every moment is "now," everywhere is "here." The individual who meets God in this way is at the center of the universe, at the crossing-point of all possible intersections.

Any encounter with God is a mind-stopping experience. Just as an encounter with something exceptionally beautiful—a sunset, a painting, a piece of music—quiets the mind momentarily so that we experience the object of our attention at a deeper level, so an encounter with God is accompanied by a quieting of the mind. It is here we begin to experience the silence of God's speech.

The sanctification of time occurs when we offer the present moment to God. We are not able to offer the past or the future, only the present moment.

The function of time in church is mainly to focus our attention on the eternity in which God lives. Thus from the moment when the priest defines worship at the beginning of the Divine Liturgy as "the Kingdom," we are no longer in ordinary time and space but in eternity, in the eternal "now" where time and space, dates, years, and seasons all exist together in the present moment. Ideally, our clocks and watches should stop working altogether until we re-emerge into the world at the end of the service.

There are many examples of prayers in which the priest invites God to join "then" with "now" (for example, in the prayers of the Blessing of the Waters at Epiphany). We, the body of Christ in a particular space and time, are brought into direct and personal contact with the saving events of Christ, many of which took place almost two thousand years ago and thousands of miles away. In that position we are also in the presence of, and meet, every member of the Church of every age and time.

Scientific time exists, and scientists are called to examine what it means, just as they are invited to examine and learn about the whole of God's creation. However, Church time, or liturgical time, also exists, measured by those who are called to be the children of God, and understood not so much with the knowledge of the head but with the wisdom of the heart.

God does not live in time. God lives in something we term variously "eternity," "everlasting life," or "the kingdom of heaven." Although we use these expressions often, we may have no clear awareness of what we are actually saying or what these expressions mean.

Even in our prayer life, we use conventions to soften the uncomfortable reality that because we live so deeply within the mystery of time, we can have little real notion of what words like "eternal" mean. Almost every prayer in the Orthodox Church ends "now and forever, and to the ages of ages, amen." Whether in Greek or Slavonic, or in any number of modern translations, this expression does not bear a great deal of meaning. Certainly the Greek word *aion* with its strong multilayered meanings gives a broader sense than the English word "age." Nevertheless, even in Greek the meaning is not clear; the Greek phrase merely points with more precision than our own tongue to a state we know we are unable to understand.

This often-repeated yet awkward expression underlines the fact that we are trying to use words to describe something beyond our words—a state of being beyond and outside our own state of being. To describe the state outside of time in which God lives is as difficult a task for us as describing God Himself, a task which the Church has generally preferred to approach with negative rather than positive language. Thus, in the convention so beloved in Eastern Christian tradition, it is easier to say what God is not than to say what God actually is.

~: CYCLES OF TIME IN THE SERVICES :~

Instead of recoiling from the task of entering time, however, the Orthodox Church dives into the temporal realm with a sense of tremendous power. If one is fortunate enough to attend the full round of services, in the form usually served only in monasteries, it is unlikely that one would attend exactly the same service more than once in a given lifetime. One of the reasons for this is that there are so many levels of time occurring simultaneously. The main result of this process is that each moment in creation is marked as liturgically unique, yet each has its own indelible sanctification.

The most obvious form of time we meet in a service is likely to be the time of day, but even here the Church has something important to say: The day starts not at the logical time of daybreak (logical, at least in the thought of a Westerner), but in the evening. At night, we see the new light of evening, the light that never fails, the light of eternal life. Like the Jewish roots of so much Orthodox tradition, the Byzantines counted time from sundown; such a system of counting time is still preserved in Mount Athos in its fullness, to the ongoing confusion of most visitors.

Thereafter, the day is sanctified by different prayers at different times—evening, night, dawn, and at the "watches" of the day. According to whether a given day is a feast day, a fast day, or an "ordinary" day (of which there are relatively few), these prayers are recited earlier or later, and mealtimes are adjusted accordingly.

The next cycle is that of the seven-day week, also of Jewish origin. This cycle's significance is made all the more mystical by the fact that the Day of the Lord, far from being a Christian Sabbath, is regarded as the eighth day of the week as well as the first. It exists within time and outside it. "Saturday" is *Savvato* in Greek, which clearly demonstrates that the Sabbath is Saturday for Orthodox Christians as much as it is for Orthodox Jews. Of course, Orthodox Christians are not bound by Old Testament Law on the subject. Within the weekly cycle, each day of the week has its own patterns, with Sunday being most distinctive, Saturday in second place, and then of the others Wednesday and Friday most marked by particular prayers.

The next cycle, in terms of length, is the eight-week cycle of the *Ochtoechos* or *Parakletiki*, the series of hymns that governs the entire tenor of the services of each week, one for each of the eight tones of Byzantine music. Each tone has its own personality, which it lends to our prayers. However, since most days also have a number of hymns and prayers in honor of the saint or saints of that particular day of the year, this musical personality is often lost. Perhaps Orthodox of future ages may choose to cut down on the special services for the saints, and thereby regain the original character of time and a greater awareness of the solemnity and importance of God's ordinary days.

The next cycle, the most elliptical in style, is only reflected in the services on the Lord's Day. That is the eleven-week cycle of the Gospel at Matins. Unnoticed by those who do not attend that service, these readings, eleven in number, bring us back time and time again to the central event of our faith, Christ's Resurrection, regarded in eleven different ways. The hymns that accompany each reading bring depth and clarity to that significance.

The penultimate cycle, mentioned already, is based on the 365 days of the year and is almost entirely devoted to the memory of the saints. Since every day of the year now commemorates many different saints, these services have grown a great deal over the years. Now each month has a special book, the *Menaion*, which governs the prayers and hymns for that particular month.

The last cycle is that of Pascha. This great day, this Feast of Feasts, like a huge comet traveling through the solar system, bends and distorts time like nothing else. Its presence in the year, weaving in and out of ordinary time based on factors which include not only the movement of the moon, but also the religious observance of the kinsmen of our Lord, attracts a number of other important days to its wake. Dominating the year, yet in many ways independent of it, Pascha stands as a fanfare of God's majestic entrance into the realm of humanity, sealing and enlivening the Incarnation of Christ in order to transform and transfigure the lives of men and women with the intensity of His love.

∾: TIME IN THE LIFE OF THE CHURCH :∾

One might expect time to act in the same way at every point on the planet, given the necessary adjustment for the movement of the sun. However, in reality this is not so. Time in Germany behaves quite differently from, say, time in Mexico. There are cultural as well as scientific forces at work.

I was reminded of this most forcibly one night when I was staying at the Monastery of St. John on the Island of Patmos in Greece. I was a deacon at the time and was due to serve at the Divine Liturgy on Sunday mornings. It was autumn and time for the clocks to change, and I thought that the hour change would take place during the night, giving me an extra hour of sleep. This would have meant getting up at 4:30 rather than 3:30 in the morning. What I did not know—at least, until someone angrily knocked on my door—was that the monastery itself does not observe the hour change. In fact, I had to get up at what was now 2:30 according to the new time to be in time for the service. Of course, everyone else in the monastery knew this fact. I did not.

Later on, I was serving a parish community in London. Most of the parishioners were from Cyprus. Cypriots, like most Greeks, have a way of dealing with time quite different from that of the average Anglo-Saxon. In this small but busy parish, I often used to have three or four baptisms, and perhaps two or three weddings, all scheduled to take place on a single Sunday afternoon. Under those circumstances, timing was crucial, since there were often large numbers of invited guests. If they had all been Greek Cypriot, there would have been no problem. The problem was that many parishioners also had English friends they wanted to invite.

It was standard practice to print invitations for a wedding, for example, but to put a time which was up to an hour earlier than the time intended in order to get the Cypriots there on time. Thus, if a wedding was to be at 4:30, the invitations might read 4:00 or even 3:30. However, this same invitation was also sent to the English guests. These would often turn up not at the time on the invitation, but early, due to the English attitude that if you are not ten minutes early, you're late. The result was that not only did the English people turn up twenty minutes early and the Greek people an hour late, but the English guests were often present for the wrong wedding!

In my own dealings with the parish, I would sometimes announce a time and then say *"Angliki ora,"* meaning "English time." In other words, the event would start "on time" in my view, though not necessarily in theirs. They put up with a lot.

Of course, ethnic differences are not the only odd feature encountered when looking at the subject of time in the Church. The Orthodox Church as a whole uses time in unexpected ways. In the Russian tradition, for example, it is common to thank God for showing us light on Saturday evenings, rather than at dawn on Sunday, to which the prayer at the end of Matins more obviously refers. The whole Orthodox Church tends to celebrate the Presanctified Liturgy—which is basically the service of Evening Prayer joined to Holy Communion—in the morning, even though the prayers clearly refer to evening time. In Holy Week, we bring almost all the services forward, singing morning services on the previous evening and evening services on the preceding morning. In monasteries, it is common practice to group services together—that is what we, as Orthodox, do.

Just as icons show liturgical reality and not necessarily historical reality, so the Church's use of time has more to do with the inner rhythms of her life than with the time expressed on clocks and watches. Demanding that all services go back to their original times is not always as sensible as it seems. The actual life of the Church, not necessarily what the books state, is what constitutes the tradition of the Church, whether universal or local.

⌒: BLESSING THE PRESENT MOMENT :⌒

Jewish tradition has a wonderful system of blessings, *berachot*, which are used on various occasions to sanctify time. They are among the first prayers Jewish children learn, and they accompany a person through life. The purpose of the blessings is multilayered. At one level, they are simply exclamations of the goodness of God. At another, they bring the greatness of God into one's awareness, making a particular moment a unique and powerful bridge between earth and heaven.

Some of the blessings are said often, others rarely. The rabbis took great care to make sure that the blessings were said in the right way, and there was a strong sense that blessings were not to be said unnecessarily. Since the name of God is used in the blessings, it was thought to be irreverent to "waste" a blessing.

At certain prayer times, these blessings now appear one after another in Jewish prayer books. However, each blessing originated deep within the Jewish soul as a comment on a particular action. Thus, "Blessed are you, Lord our God, King of the universe, who gave us bread from the earth" is the blessing that accompanies the breaking of bread. Indeed, when the New Testament writers say that Jesus took bread and blessed it, these may have been precisely the words He used.

There are blessings for performing certain actions, such as washing hands or putting on clothing; others which are recited on seeing beautiful sights in nature; and yet others which are said on special occasions, such as seeing a king or meeting a great sage. There is one blessing that is only recited on occasions when a person feels he or she has been rescued from death.

In the Orthodox Church, we hear an echo of these Jewish blessings at the beginning of every service, when the priest says, "Blessed is our God, always, now and forever and to the ages of ages, amen." Announcing the blessedness of God is not simply stating the obvious: "God is blessed." Rather it has the effect of making that moment in time the bearer of blessing: time itself becomes a blessing.

This is the way most prayers start in the Church. It is in this way that regular time is transformed into special time and the regular moment into a bearer of blessing. The prayers of the Church, like the chiming of a clock, proclaim the presence of the present moment. Each proclaims the sanctity of God and the sanctity of the moment.

There is one more blessing the Church uses in this way, but only once a day. This occurs at the beginning of the main morning prayers, the Orthros service, or is moved to the beginning of an all-night vigil, of which the morning prayers are a major part. "Glory to the Holy, Consubstantial, Life-giving and Undivided Trinity, always, now and forever and to the ages of ages, amen."

Here we have a sense that the Church is remembering the old Jewish dictum about not wasting blessings. God is described fully, yet with clarity and succinctness. One gets the feeling that although this proclamation occurs only once each day, nevertheless it is enough. The statement is complete because it describes not only the Godhead, but also our relationship with the Godhead. We must proclaim "glory" in order for the relationship—that between the members of the Holy Trinity and that between the Holy Trinity and us—to be put into motion. The members of the Trinity constantly express their love for each other, and we, together with the hosts of heaven, acknowledge their holiness and proclaim their glory.

These first two blessings, exalted and profound as they are, describe ordinary time, the time of the eternal passage of the present moment from hour to hour, day to day, and year to year. However, when the Church wants to celebrate a Mystery, one of those events in which regular time is replaced with eternal time, the blessing is different. Instead of the beginning, "Blessed is our God," we use the blessing, "Blessed is the Kingdom of the Father and of the Son and of the Holy Spirit, now and forever and to the ages of ages, amen."

Here several things happen at once. Firstly, God is addressed in His fullness, in the Trinity. The Trinity is not a teaching anyone finds easy to understand—indeed it is perhaps more correct to say that the Trinity is itself a mystery, not something any one of us should expect to fully comprehend. However, one thing we can say is that the Trinity gives a sense of dimension to God, and the relationship between the three members of the Trinity provides a sense of movement. This is a dynamic God, not some impersonal power poised at some distant point in the universe. This is a God who contains relationship within Himself. Although He is complete within Himself, nevertheless He chooses to extend that relationship towards the universe He has created. In particular, He extends that relationship towards the creature whose very humanity has been taken up into the Godhead through the Incarnation of the Son of God.

When the Church uses this longer blessing, she expects God to intervene in a direct and immediate manner. She expects God to reveal Himself in His action within the Mystery being celebrated. She expects a revelation to take place, just as God revealed Himself to Adam, to Abraham, and to Moses. Once a revelation takes place, the world is different, and the people involved are never the same again.

When the priest proclaims, "Blessed is the Kingdom," he is not so much talking of the destination of the Church at that moment, but rather making eternal life present and available to everyone there.

~: CHAPTER 6 :~

Sacred Places for Sacred People

In English, as in Greek, we often use the word "church" to signify a particular building. However, the deepest significance of that word refers not to a building but to the people who worship in it. The whole point of the church building is to provide the members of the Body of Christ with the right space in which to experience the presence of God. Everything in the building, inside and outside, should be aimed at assisting the worshipper to get into focus and to keep in focus, from the moment she or he enters the door.

Architecture is at the service of this process, and the traditional forms of Orthodox architecture, though different in different countries, tend to produce a single line of vision: The Divine Liturgy is the proclamation of the Kingdom of heaven; the church building is the sacred space that encourages and enhances that proclamation.

~: WHO WE ARE IN CHURCH :~

From the moment a person enters the door of the church, whether rich or poor, an aged archbishop or a young neophyte, he or she goes through a sort of inner transformation in order to meet God. We act and feel in a different way when we are in a sacred space; in some sense, we might even talk of being different people when we are in church. Most often, our voices tend to get quieter, our movements less hurried; our sense of being present grows rather than diminishes. Our minds may calm down or they may not, but there is an overwhelming sense that they are invited to do so.

When we see someone else behaving like an "outside person" inside the church building, we instinctively know and feel that it is not right. Much of the time, children respond instinctively to their surroundings and make adjustments to their behavior accordingly. It is only when they "forget" that they are in church that we need to direct them to be quiet.

We enter church as complete persons. We need to be aware how unworthy we are to enter the presence of God, and many of the prayers of preparation for Holy Communion direct us precisely to this sense of unworthiness. We are unworthy, and there is nothing we can do to rectify the situation. It is only by God's grace that we can enter the Presence without coming to harm.

At the same time, we have to come to terms with our own sacredness. This is often more difficult than being aware of our unworthiness. This sacredness is associated with our most profound sense of being. When we are present before God, we stand as if our potential had already been realized and we were now taking our places in the Kingdom yet to come.

Feelings of distance from God mix with feelings of belonging to Him. As we stand in church at the Divine Liturgy, we are simultaneously Adam knocking on the gates of Paradise, and the prodigal son being received back into full communion as a fully accepted member of the family of heaven.

We have to learn not to shrink from this paradox, this seeming contradiction between who we are and who God sees us to be. Paradox always presents a great opportunity for growth. The lack of any sign of making sense is a powerful reminder to the individual to put aside the methods of the mind (which we normally use to solve problems) and to sit quietly in the heart, seeking neither solution nor satisfaction. When we come to paradox, then, we have to proceed with courage, but a courage tinged with humility. This humility has nothing to do with humiliation, which is the mark of the defeated; rather, it is the proud

The Greek word for church, *ekklesia,* carries a strong connotation of being chosen. It is difficult to come to terms with being chosen. In the end, it has nothing to do with being superior to anyone else, which is what our minds invariably want us to believe. Rather, it has to do with having a strong sense of responsibility, of mission and purpose. The members of the Body of Christ are both called and chosen.

We must always remember that God does not need a church building to live in. This truth is in direct contrast to the idea behind the Greek temples of the classical era. More like a Jewish synagogue, the church building is there for us, to help us achieve encounter with God. It is we, not God, who need the building. God is everywhere present, filling all things.

For us, however, particularly in the beginning of our spiritual lives, it is difficult to meet God anywhere and everywhere. We sometimes have to ask Him to remove Himself or to postpone His presence until we are ready. We do that by asking Him to meet us in the church.

Although we are never actually out of the presence of God, we are seldom ready to be in it. Even with all the complexity of Orthodox architecture and liturgy around us, we are still not ready in any real sense, but we are at least expecting an encounter to take place. It may be that in the course of our training we will get more used to being in the Presence and actually get better at encountering God in other places, as well as in the church. However, most of us never leave the ranks of spiritual beginners, and we can expect to be taking baby steps for much of our lives.

~: THE PARTS OF THE CHURCH BUILDING :~

The Steps

We sometimes enter a church by walking up steps, and some of the most sacred sites of Christianity are built in or on high places. The action of ascent is the beginning of the process of our inner transformation. It makes us aware that we are going somewhere special, even though the nature of the special place is not yet apparent.

Many buildings designed for legal or ceremonial use have steps, sometimes on a huge scale. The Capitol in Washington, DC, has grand and beautiful steps. In the courts of many kings and queens, including the emperors of Byzantium, the ruler sat on a throne that had to be approached by steps. In everyday speech, we "look up" to authority, and we "look down" on those we reckon to be inferior to ourselves.

Within the tradition of Eastern Orthodoxy, the idea of height has great significance, and this is hardly surprising. Jesus Himself often went up a hillside to pray, and for our spiritual ancestors, the Jews, going to the temple in Jerusalem was a matter of ascending, since Jerusalem sits on high ground.

What many regard as our most sacred monastic center, Athos, is actually a group of monasteries gathered around a mountain. Indeed, in Greek, the normal way to refer to Athos is as *Agion Oros*, the Holy Mountain.

On the island of Patmos, where St. John wrote down the Revelation which bears his name, the monastery, for spiritual as well as tactical reasons, was built at the highest point on the island. Arriving in the courtyard of the monastery gives the pilgrim a sense of accomplishment. One way or another, you have ascended a height that looks quite daunting from down in the village, where the boats come in.

Mount Sinai, and the Monastery of St. Catherine at its foot, stands as another example of a place where we, as a race, have literally climbed upwards in order to encounter God. (Of course, no one in the modern world would consider that we could be nearer God by climbing a mountain, any more than anyone would think that walking to the front of the plane would get him to his destination faster. Nevertheless, the psychological effect of height remains powerful.)

The Narthex

Having climbed the steps, we open the door of the church, and we continue to go through this important transformation. We cease gradually to be the people that we are out in the street. That is to say, we stop being regular people and start to take on the attributes of our "identity within the Mystery," which is, in a sense, our true identity—as members of the people of God. This identity is given to us in Holy Baptism, and the first part of the church we enter is the narthex, the place where the Holy Mystery of Baptism has its rightful place.

Back in the first Christian centuries, at the time when the Church had to be on guard against people stealing its sacred secrets, candidates for baptism were not allowed to see the place of the liturgy until after they were baptized. We need to re-experience that moment of first introduction each time we walk through the narthex and into the body of the church. As Christians, we are forever invited to be new, to be remade, to start again. Although this renewal belongs properly to the Holy Mystery of Confession, it also happens each time we enter the sacred space of Orthodox worship.

The Nave and Sanctuary

One feature of note in Orthodox church buildings is that, unlike many Western churches, the function of the architecture is not to reach up to heaven so much as to allow heaven to come to earth. We rarely see spires soaring upwards, straining to reach somewhere beyond our ability to go. Rather, the domes and arches of classical Orthodox architecture encourage a sense of "heaven on earth." Far from this being an experience for which we wait until the end of time, the Divine Liturgy provides us with a present experience of the Kingdom of heaven.

In the main body of the church building, the most notable feature is probably the icon screen that stands towards the eastern end of the church. The screen forms a wall between the nave, where the people stand, and the sanctuary—the Holy of Holies, the place of the altar, the throne of God.

Several times a year, groups of schoolchildren come to visit our church—for a variety of reasons. One question I often ask, particularly of those children who have never been into a church like ours before, is, "What is the most important part of the church?" Almost invariably, the children point towards the holy table, even though they cannot see it, since it is behind the icon screen and the doors of the screen are shut.

There is a common understanding, even among those who are both innocent and ignorant, that the eastern end, where the altar stands, is the sacred end of the church. A consequence of this basic configuration is that the sense of sacredness decreases as we walk towards the west. Here again, this is a convenience for us—there is no place where God is absent, and certainly He is no less present at the western door of the church than He is in the altar area.

Sometimes people ask me if it is not lonely for the priest to stand in the sanctuary beyond the icon screen. I think most priests would agree with me when I say that is absolutely not the case. If anything, being "in the altar" (the expression we generally use for being in the area behind the screen), one is all the more acutely aware of the presence not only of the people, with whom one is in almost constant dialogue, but also of those in attendance we cannot see: angels and archangels, the saints and friends of God who crowd around the Presence in countless numbers.

In its present form, the icon screen makes it difficult, if not impossible, for most people to see the altar clearly. For Western people, nourished on a steady diet of seeking wisdom through the mind, this might present something of a problem. Gradually, though, as one adapts to the rhythms and textures of Orthodox worship, it becomes apparent that it is not necessarily beneficial to be able to see exactly what is happening at the altar. After all, what happens there is sacred, but it is not a secret. Under certain circumstances, it is quite permissible to celebrate the Divine Liturgy without an icon screen—as was the practice, of course, in the early periods of the history of the church. St. John Chrysostom never saw anything like the icon screens to which we are accustomed.

The icon screen points us in many directions at once. We may think of it as the barrier between earth and heaven, which at certain times in the service are united and made real to each other through the actions of the priest, the deacon, and the people. The deacons, in particular, fly like angels from earth to heaven, uniting the seen with the unseen, their wings flapping around them.

A deacon is an important feature of the Orthodox liturgy, and it is regrettable that so many parishes, particularly in the United States, rarely see a deacon in action. His role of not-quite-layman, not-quite-priest gives him a unique and important task. Indeed, at a liturgy in which a bishop is celebrating, it is the deacons, together with the bishop, who actively conduct the service, the priests being relegated to a somewhat ceremonial and supportive role.

Another important contrast provided by the icon screen reaches back beyond the earliest days of the Church. In Jewish tradition, before the destruction of the temple in AD 70, the functions of the temple and the synagogue were entirely separate. The temple was the place of the Presence and the place of sacrifice. It was organized and run by priests, and the rites and prayers were regulated by an intense sense of ritual purity, as outlined in the Torah. Since the time of David and Solomon, there had been a strong, though somewhat idealized, tradition that Jerusalem was unique and that there could be only one temple. It was to this temple that the people went up three times a year. Jesus Himself was taken there a number of times as a child, and spent much of His last days teaching and preaching there.

A synagogue, on the other hand, was essentially a place of meeting and study. (In Hebrew, synagogues are actually called "houses of study." The word "synagogue" is Greek, indicating a place where people meet.) A synagogue was not the domain of the priests, but of lay teachers called rabbis. There were many synagogues scattered all over the Jewish world. They were the place of the people and supremely the place of the Torah, the books of the Law.

Thus, in the Orthodox Church, we can see strands of both of these Jewish traditions. The altar area represents the temple of old with its priests, its place of sacrifice, its deep sense of Presence. The nave more clearly reflects a synagogue, the place of the Book (since it is here that Scripture is proclaimed), the place of the people. If the altar represents the power of the priests (hierarchy), the influence of lay people predominates in the nave. The place of the altar is quiet and intense. The nave, on the other hand, is less ordered, more democratic, less formal, noisier, less refined.

For Orthodox Christians, the church building is supremely itself during the celebration of the Divine Liturgy. Use of the altar area at services other than the liturgy merely reflects the core experience of the liturgy itself, as the moon reflects the light of the sun. Almost all the ceremonial actions of the Orthodox Church at prayer can be clearly seen as having been derived directly from the liturgy. Throughout the whole day, the altar table, as the Throne of God, is the focus of our attention. However, it really comes into its own when the sacred tablecloth, the *antimension*, is opened during the liturgy, and the table becomes at once an altar of sacrifice and the table of the banquet of the Kingdom of heaven.

∾ BEING PRESENT IN THE LITURGY ∾

Another purpose of the icon screen, which does not at first appear particularly obvious, is to assist in heightening the awareness of the people. This is most noticeable during the Divine Liturgy when, according to the old custom, the holy doors are closed while the clergy receive Holy Communion. The doors are closed, the curtain is drawn, and the priest quietly prays a beautiful prayer of preparation for Communion. The deacon then exclaims, "Let us attend!" There is nothing to hear, nothing to see, and yet the deacon exclaims, "Pay attention!"

It is precisely because at this point our senses are of no use to us that the tension of this puzzle is so important. At this point, we are encouraged to experience the presence directly—not by seeing, since there is nothing to see; not by understanding, since there is nothing to understand—but by being, simply being in the presence of God.

The Fathers talk of an active, intense awareness called *nepsis*. This nepsis can occur right here in the liturgy when, for a moment, our minds go quiet (for there is nothing in particular for them to do), and we freely and intently stand in the presence of God. The doors and the veil remind us that what is to be seen in heaven makes no sense to our physical eyes: we cannot see God in the physical sense. If we want to see Him, we have to seek Him on a higher plane—at a higher level of awareness, not with our eyes.

One of the most important features of Orthodox worship is that it engages all of our senses. It does not seek to be an intellectual exercise—very little about our relationship with God depends on our knowledge, wisdom, or understanding. It is more to do with us being aware, being present, being receptive.

This factor is assisted by the way the services are put together. Sounds surround us, we smell the incense and the sweet smell of the candles and lamps burning, we move around lighting the candles, kissing the icons, we are bombarded with visual images: the frescoes, the vestments, the lights, the movements of the ministers and our fellow worshippers. These are not distractions—these are the experience of worship.

Where we so easily fall short of the ideal of Orthodox worship is in using the time to think about other things—about problems at work, or what we are going to have for dinner, or some unkindness we shared with a stranger last week, or what a boss said yesterday or might say tomorrow. At that moment, we see the icons, hear the choir, smell the incense, and we come back to reality, and stand once more in the court of heaven.

The actions of Orthodox worshippers, as well as those of the ministers, are aimed at keeping us focused and keeping us present. The act of lighting a candle is a powerful and spiritual gesture. Light is life, and whenever we bring light into darkness, we are reminded of God. The candle, of course, just burns. It does not start doing something else or wondering if it should be somewhere else. That is how we should be, at least while we are in church. We punctuate our prayers with the sign of the cross, and each time we do so we bring ourselves back to the Throne, no matter how powerfully our minds are pulling us this way and that.

Prayer is not easy, but the role of the church building is to make that task a little easier. The Orthodox community comes closest to experiencing heaven during the Divine Liturgy, and it is the role of the building to bring that experience to life.

~: CHAPTER 7 :~

Icons & the Incarnation

*I*CONS ARE ART FOR THE HEART.

For the human mind, an icon is so-and-so tall by such-and-such wide, painted this way or that, by a certain person, according to the traditions of a particular school, and it is worth a certain amount, based on the knowledge (or lack of it) of the viewer. The mind looks at an icon and immediately compares it with other icons, describes its features, labels its qualities.

The heart, by contrast, simply resonates voicelessly with the spiritual reality portrayed upon the icon's surface.

Western art on the one hand, and icons on the other, generally seek different reactions from the viewer. Most Western pictures, particularly those of religious subjects, draw out an emotional reaction from the viewer—compassion, sadness, wonderment. Icons do not. An icon invites the believer to dive more deeply into the mystery.

Some icons are exceptionally beautiful, others less so. Some are national treasures and world-renowned works of art. Others, equally important, are postcards mounted on pieces of plywood, almost hidden in dusty corners. All depict holy people or sacred occasions, and most are painted or presented in a form that demonstrates their identity with little or no doubt.

In Russia and among some pietist groups of Greece, Western paintings have sometimes been used as icons. This presents a number of spiritual problems, since they are essentially different in their tasks—not better or worse, just different. Compare a religious painting by Rembrandt, for example, with an icon by Rublev. Once realized, the difference is very apparent, even though both are artistic masterpieces. Each seeks to achieve a different end. (To allow this difference a greater context, the paintings of El Greco present an interesting halfway point and may be seen to have characteristics from both sides.)

For the Church, an icon communicates a spiritual reality directly to the person who views it. This communication does not depend on any particular wisdom or knowledge on the part of the viewer, but rather on his or her degree of spiritual awareness and openness.

Icons have a great deal to say about the relationship between God and the world He created. This relationship, and our understanding of it, needs to be looked at before we can make much progress.

~: THE ICON AS A SAFEGUARD AGAINST HERESY :~

Throughout history, the human spirit has periodically shown a tendency to want to distance the Creator from creation. Plato exemplified this tendency four hundred years before Christ, as did the gnostics in the second century, the Manicheans in the fourth, the Cathars in the thirteenth, and in a general way the puritans of every age. In this frame of mind, God is a spirit and must remain uncontaminated by the ephemeral quality of life as we know it.

Parallel with this way of thinking is a deeply rooted distrust many of us feel toward our own bodies—particularly in those aspects of human life that remind us of our common nature with the animal kingdom. We have a tendency to try to exclude God from those areas of life, even though to attempt to shut God out of anything is utterly futile.

Compounding this tendency is another that places fashion before function. In almost every age, certainly among the rich, fashion has demanded that our bodies, both male and female, be shaped other than the way they are. The glossy goddesses in magazines look very different from the women we see in shops, planes, and churches. This makes the woman on the street distrustful of herself. In general, we—men as well as women—don't much like the way our bodies look. Part of the natural psychological baggage we carry around is this rejection of reality in favor of the idealized and sanitized body-image perpetuated by Hollywood.

No wonder, then, that we find it difficult to see our own bodies as the work of the Creator, since we have a deep, keen awareness that our bodies are flawed. "Let us leave God to the Ideals (as in Plato's thinking), but keep Him away from me," becomes the cry of the human race.

This strong sense of an immense division between God and creation is, in some people, accompanied by a strong sense of right and wrong and an all-or-nothing or black-and-white way of thinking. In the pure spirit world, good is good and evil is evil. You have to choose. However, in reality, we almost always live in shades of grey, a fact which does not please the puritan mindset. According to this way of thinking, complication is scorned, as is subtlety. Narrow-mindedness and denial, often in an attempt to shut out difficult or unpleasant aspects of life, are valued and promoted. Unrealistic views of history, idealizing a particular age when "all was well," are created and promulgated. Norms and ideals that differ from those accepted by the majority are dismissed out of hand as being alien and probably evil. God is good; the world outside the immediate family is desperately evil and must be distrusted. God and His world must be kept separate.

Plato and those who followed his teachings (including Plotinus, who developed a philosophy called neo-Platonism, which found great favor in certain parts of the Church) went so far as to introduce, as a matter of philosophical necessity, a being intermediate between God and the creation. Plato thought that God, like everything completely real and authentic, had to be spirit. Therefore, God had to use an agent, whom Plato called a "creator" (in Greek *demiourgos*, which leads to the rather comical English word "demiurge"), in order to create the world, since God could not sully His being with matter. God is perfect and thus changeless. The world of reality is forever changing, and therefore cannot belong to God.

The whole notion that God is completely separate from His creation, and that matter is inherently less than perfect and therefore to be avoided as much as possible, is entirely alien to Orthodox Christian tradition, and the icon bears significant silent witness to this fact. The words of the Gospel are uncompromising: "In the beginning was the Word . . . and the Word became flesh." Not only does the Word become flesh, but He is also the agent of creation; "all things were made through Him" (John 1:1, 3, 14). This is the Word of God, the second Person of the Holy Trinity, who was in time to become Jesus. Perfect God, but also perfect man, Jesus is no secondary creative power necessitated by the application of a theory, but God-made-man, the theanthropic Savior.

(It is interesting to note that the word which describes Jesus becoming a human being is given a slightly different sense in Western languages [affected by Latin] from that which is understood in the languages of Orthodoxy. The Latin word *incarnatio* [from which we get "incarnation"] actually means something like "enfleshment." The Greek word that *incarnatio* translates is *enanthropoisis*, or "enhumanment.")

Thus, by extension, the existence of icons as supporters of our spiritual life proclaims the Incarnation of Christ. The Word made flesh fills all of creation with His presence, and thus the physical world starts its long transformation into the Kingdom.

~: ICONS AS GOD-BEARERS :~

It may seem a long way from the Incarnation (or "enhumanment") of the Son of God to the Church's awareness of icons, but they are actually both on the same path. Once we have a strong sense that God is willing and able to enter into the world He Himself created—rather than stand outside and observe it, as a clock maker might watch his creation—then we have to face the ability of created matter, the stuff that surrounds us all the time, to be "God-bearing," and not only in some symbolic way.

An important example of this awareness takes place in the Divine Liturgy. When we present the bread and wine (called, in Orthodoxy, the gifts) at the beginning of the service, they are like icons of Christ. We treat them with great reverence, much as we might treat a highly revered icon. However, at this point they are simply a piece of bread and some wine. When, later in the service, the Church (through the words spoken by the priest) asks God to change them from bread and wine into the Body and Blood of the Lord, the bread and wine cease to be "merely" an icon and start being the Body and Blood in every way.

The fact that this can happen without a tremendous explosion taking place on the holy table is due, here also, to the "enhumanment" of Jesus. One way of describing this paradox, both in the Bible and in the writings of the great saints of the Church, is that Jesus "emptied Himself" in an act of great humility. He put aside His power (not "doing" power so much as "being" power) so that He would be able to live among us without causing us harm.

So, icons are God-bearing pieces of creation, a creation made by God in the first place but somehow tainted, its spiritual quality made less obvious through the great tragedy we call the Fall. However, since God became man, this same material, through the work of the forester, the carpenter, the paint-maker, and eventually the icon painter, is returned to the fullness of its spiritual origins in a way most of the stuff that surrounds us is not. Icons are Spirit-bearing in a way that, for example, automobiles cannot be (at least not yet).

Icons, then, are not pictures in any accepted sense. The styles favored most by the Church throughout history are those in which the person depicted is recognizable, but the portrayal is in no sense photographic. To start with, the imagery is two-dimensional, certain dimensions are elongated, and the perspective is not geometric. If one were to cut out the figure portrayed, it would not stand up.

An icon as a flat surface is something we do not so much look at as look through. However, the expression "windows into heaven" is a little misleading perhaps, since icons actually invite us to enter the mystery rather than to look beyond using our imagination.

Icons are a perpetual reminder that we do not require an image of who God is in our imaginations. The exact details in icons may be the result of the Church's collective experience, but that is far removed from the egocentric imagination of the individual. It is interesting, though, that the Church has never said that one icon or another is the correct or real icon of Christ. Moreover, the awareness of the icon painter is never lacking in the icon, even in the most traditional setting. There is always a resonance between the art as form and the personality of the icon painter.

According to the books, icons are best painted by people who are fasting, praying, and living exemplary lives, preferably in monasteries. However, if you visit Orthodox countries, you will also see fine icons being painted by men in shop-front studios, cigarette in mouth, with seemingly little regard for the spirituality all around them.

In the end, an icon is a good icon because it most clearly expresses the experience of the Church, no matter the source. In a more daring manner, the same can be said of doctrinal writing and thinking in general. Dogmatic theology did not descend from heaven, but rather started in the hearts and minds of men and women who then shared their ideas with others. Some of their work accurately described the experience of the saints; some of it did not. The former is doctrine; the latter is heresy. That is the criterion by which the Orthodox Church lives. The decisions of the Ecumenical Councils are important not because they came from ecumenical councils, but because they reflect the experience of the saints.

Icons do not necessarily portray historical reality, but they do portray spiritual reality. They sometimes present paradox, upsetting to the human mind but quite acceptable to the nous. St. John the Forerunner is sometimes depicted as an angel standing next to a platter that contains his head. St. Christopher is given the head of a dog. In the typical Byzantine icon of the Nativity, Jesus appears more than once. The angels and shepherds are there, but so are the wise men, who, according to scholars, arrived months or years later.

It might be more accurate to say that an icon is a liturgical object, and its meaning is most clear within the context of the liturgy, the divine acting-out of our salvation. Outside that context, it loses most, though not all, of its impact. To remove an icon entirely from the life of the Church robs it of all its spiritual dynamism. Placing an icon in an art gallery is a matter of spiritual shame—until, of course, the icon transforms the gallery into a church, as sometimes happened in the former Soviet Union.

In Orthodox tradition we are not encouraged to stare at icons, to contemplate them. When used in prayer, they are not the objects of devotion, but simply a center of presence. The devotion belongs beyond the icon, and the veneration of the icon is always the veneration of the person or event depicted on it.

Once prepared and blessed, the icon remains a protrusion of eternity, of the Kingdom, into the present world. The icon, unlike a human person, cannot ever be less than it is—an icon cannot sin, nor can it mar its own image of God in the same way that human beings can do so readily. Icons, then, are a guarantee, in a sense, of the relationship between God and the world.

PART II

The Mysteries of the Church ❧

~: CHAPTER 8 :~

Birth & Baptism

O**N OR AROUND THE FORTIETH DAY AFTER A CHILD IS** born, following the path taken by the Lord and His blessed Mother, the mother of a newborn child presents herself and her child at the door of the church. There she is welcomed by the priest, and the congregation if possible. Prayers are said that consist of blessings for the mother and the child, welcoming the mother back into the full communion of the Church now that she has completed the holy and life-giving task of childbirth.

These prayers, together with some of the Church's traditional practices around the act of childbirth (as well as the menstrual cycle), are based on attitudes which have largely disappeared from Western society and sometimes cause people to wonder. These particular attitudes, which have their roots firmly within Jewish tradition, have as their general foundation a deep and mysterious understanding of the relationship between life and blood.

The key to understanding and coming to terms with these attitudes lies in the fact that Jewish tradition made little distinction between things that were unclean because they were dirty or soiled and things that were unclean because they were too holy to touch. Texts of Holy Scripture and dead bodies were both capable of imparting this sense of impurity, but the most significant substance in this regard is almost certainly blood. Even a quick perusal of some of the sections of the

Old Testament regarding ritual purity reveals that blood not only has a very interesting symbolism of its own (which for Orthodox Christians finds its highest expression in the words of Jesus at the Mystical Supper), but also connects some major themes that run through Jewish and Christian tradition: life and death, marriage and birth, sacrifice and redemption, sin and forgiveness.

The notion of impurity in the Jewish sense, which means that something or someone is barred from participation in temple worship, carries no automatic sense of being morally or physically impure. It has context and meaning in terms of temple worship which has been lost in the modern world.

The state of a woman after childbirth is that she is impure in a ritual sense, not through being dirty or unclean, but because she is too holy. She has participated in the co-creation of a human life and has thus worked closely with God during the process of childbirth, from early pregnancy until well after the child is born. This places her in a unique and significant spiritual condition.

This tradition was taken into the life of the Orthodox Church in a fairly complete form, even though most other Jewish ritual legislation concerning marital relations was not. A young mother is encouraged to stay at home with her child for the forty days following birth and, as such, she is excluded from worshipping with the rest of the Christian community.[12]

However, this exclusion is no punishment. Rather, releasing her from her obligation, as a member of the Body of Christ, to participate in the worship of the Church during these forty days allows her time to recover from the physical exertions of childbirth, as well as giving her time to bond with her new child. Welcoming her and the child at the fortieth day ends this special period for her, just as the forty-day memorial service after someone dies encourages the closest relatives of the deceased to return to everyday life.

There are a number of prayers in the church books surrounding the birth of a child. A prayer on the day of birth, together with that of naming the child on the eighth day (as Jesus Himself was named and

---

12 This tradition is not practiced in all parishes in the United States.

circumcised on the eighth day), reminds us that the entire rhythm of
birth is sanctified. The words used at the fortieth-day blessing mention the fact that the child will be brought back to church in due
course to take part in the Mystery of Holy Baptism.

Before the Mystery of Baptism can actually take place, the parents have to make an important decision, and that is to choose a godparent for their child.

The role of the godparent is actually quite complicated. He or she
has an important role to play in the baptism, particularly in cases where
the candidate is a child too young to answer for itself. In this case, the
godparent makes all the responses in the service on behalf of the baby.

The office of godparent is one that requires some comment. The
duties of the godparents are considerable, since it is ultimately they,
rather than the parents, who are responsible for the religious upbringing of the child. It is their duty to make sure that the child goes to
church frequently and receives Holy Communion at the Divine Liturgy. This is an area where there have probably been a great variety of
customs throughout the Church's history. Certainly, in the modern
world in which the nuclear family is the most common unit, the task
of taking a child to church more often falls to the parent rather than
the godparent. This makes it all the more important that a godparent
be chosen from outside the family of the child to be baptized. We
may assume that blood relations are always going to be available to
assist the child, should he or she be in need. It is in tragic circumstances where no relations are available that the role of the godparent
comes into its own.

It is always worth remembering that the relationship between
child and godparent is regarded by the Church as very important—in
fact, it is deemed as powerful as a blood relationship. In practice, this
means that the various godchildren of a godparent are related to one
another, and are therefore not able to marry each other. This is taken
so seriously in certain parts of the Church that it is common for a
person to have either godsons or goddaughters, but not both. This
solves the problem of possible intermarrying in later life.

It need hardly be stated that the godparent is expected to be, first
and foremost, a practicing member of the Orthodox Church, and

someone who will be able and willing to take his or her spiritual role seriously. The role of godparent is nothing like the role of a rich uncle or a visiting benefactor. There is nothing wrong with being either of these things, but they are not the same as being a godparent.

❦ THE SYMBOLISM OF WATER ❦

Before looking at baptism itself, let us first examine the theme of water, so central to our understanding of the symbolism involved in this, the major rite of initiation into the life of the Church.

The most delicious drink I can remember, I received while lying in a hospital bed, having just come round from a general anesthetic after surgery. I was in significant discomfort, but most of all, I was very thirsty. However, because of the anesthesia, the nurses would not give me anything to drink at that time. I waited for what seemed a very long period, drifting in and out of sleep. Eventually one of the nurses appeared and helped me to sit up. She gave me one teaspoonful of water. Although it did nothing to quench my long-term thirst, it was the most delicious drink of my entire life. It was pure pleasure.

Thirst points to a more urgent need than hunger. We thirst for water before we hunger for bread. We need water to stay alive more immediately than we need food. For members of the human race, water is not an optional extra. When it comes to sustaining our life, water is as important as the air we breathe, the pressure of air that keeps us together, and the gravity that holds us down. Water is the major covering of our planet and the main ingredient of our bodies.

All in all, water plays a crucial part in our most profound awareness of life: no water, no life. Our reality is as simple as that. When our scientists search for other planets to find life forms we might recognize, they look first for water. Without that water, there is no point in looking any further.

It is hardly surprising that God uses this substance to meet us in this initial Mystery.

As with most things that overawe us, we use a complex set of symbols connected with water: it is at once romantic, nutritious, and dangerous. It is the source of our life, but also the home of the various sea monsters that plagued our nightmares long before the psalmist sang the praises of Leviathan or the elves crossed the sea to leave Middle Earth. The life-giving liquid is also a killer, powerful and relentless, drowning all in its path. Things in wells, floods, shipwrecks, accidental drowning—these are all part of our relationship with water, as much as are the cooling glass of lemonade, the brook running through the meadow on a summer's day, the oasis in the middle of a desert, the teardrop on the face of a child.

We are born in water, having been sustained, nourished, and protected by it during the important weeks in the womb before birth. Once born, we are washed in it, and then, almost immediately, we start to drink it in the form of milk. We may be born fragile and helpless, but we know how to drink. As children, we learn gradually to respect water, to have fun in it, to use it, and sometimes to avoid it. We use it to clean our environment, our possessions, and ourselves.

Purification is an important part of our religious understanding, and it is hardly surprising that there has been an almost constant connection between purification and water throughout human history. In the spiritual roots of Orthodox Christianity, purification was key to the Judaic understanding of the relationship between God and humanity.

Jewish customs of purification almost certainly had their origins in the practical demands of physical cleanliness. Presumably, washing one's hands before praying was similar to washing one's hands before eating. Over time, this process became more and more refined until the washing had little if anything to do with physical cleanliness. There was a more powerful and more profound significance in becoming ritually pure through washing, which in the end became the dominant factor. An observant Jew will set water by his bed so that he can wash his hands before moving in the morning and thus be prepared for prayer. Prayer is the most anxious need of the individual upon waking, but in Jewish thought washing is regarded as a necessary preliminary to that contact with God. The same influence can be seen when, in the Divine Liturgy, the priest washes his hands before performing his sacred task.

Washing for the sake of purification has a high priority in the life of an observant Jew. When St. John the Forerunner preached the baptism of repentance, he was not inventing something new. On the contrary, he was talking about something all the Jews of his age would have recognized. In contrast, Christians are not too concerned with the idea of ritual purity as it relates to daily cleanliness, except when it comes to baptism.

The theme of baptism in the early experience of the Christian Church makes one clear distinction from the earlier Jewish practices. For Christians, baptism was almost entirely cut off from any notion of physical cleansing. Rather, it was an action in which God makes an indelible mark in the person being baptized. The cry of the Forerunner links baptism not only with repentance, but also with the proclamation of the Kingdom. His voice has never been silenced, and even though it is more difficult to see the obvious significance of his call at the baptism of a child as opposed to an adult, nevertheless the call still rings in the ears of all the baptized.

❧ WHY DO WE BAPTIZE? ☙

The answer to that question is found towards the end of the baptismal service, after the baptism proper, after the procession around the font and the reading of the epistle. The priest reads the last four verses of St. Matthew's Gospel, which include these words addressed to His disciples, "Go therefore and make disciples of all the nations, baptizing them in the name of the Father and of the Son and of the Holy Spirit, teaching them to observe all things that I have commanded you; and lo, I am with you always, even to the end of the age" (Matthew 28:19–20).

This reading shows a great deal about what it means to be a member of the Church: it means to be a disciple, and the way to become a disciple is to be baptized in the name of the Holy Trinity. To be a disciple means to have a relationship with God that will never be taken away. This is not merely the relationship of creature and Creator. That relationship is already fixed at physical birth, and no human agent can do anything about it for good or ill. The relationship begun at baptism refers to the relationship in which the individual meets God on a personal level.

In the Church, we baptize because Jesus told us to. Like the other Mysteries, baptism is not simply a good idea which was made into a tradition of the Church. The Mysteries have been the same through good times and bad, through periods of all sorts of economic and social change, for people who were well-educated or not. The Mysteries come to us from God, and even if their significance is not always clear without some explanation, they are specifically the ways in which God chooses to approach us and teaches us to be the people He wants us to be.

In the case of baptism, we have a great deal of information contained in the various versions of Jesus' baptism in all four Gospels, even though the account in St. John's Gospel is characteristically mysterious.

Although John the Baptist declared himself to be unworthy to perform the sacred rite, he did, at Jesus' request, perform Jesus' baptism. Following the example of the sacred role model, the priest prays a beautiful quiet prayer at the beginning of the baptismal service in which he acknowledges his own unworthiness to perform the work of God.

If, at a baptism, the priest or bishop takes the part of St. John the Forerunner, the person being baptized takes the part of Jesus Himself. This is not a mere symbol, nor is it sacrilegious in any way. On the contrary, the whole point of Christian baptism is that the person being baptized should find his or her identity in the Savior. This process commences when the person identifies with Jesus in the Mystery of Baptism, and thus finds his or her identity as a member of the Body of Christ. Later, this identity grows to become the dominant and eternal part of the person's complete identity. This is the indelible mark of baptism: a person is given a new identity within the Body of Christ and starts a new, eternal life.

For this reason, an older person is often given a new name in baptism in order to mark the transition from one life to another. The newly baptized (or "neophyte," meaning "newly illumined" or "newly enlightened") is no longer merely born a child of the physical body, which is wonderful enough. He or she is now a child of the light, a child of the Kingdom. From the moment he or she emerges from the water, a new life begins—marked not by physical characteristics, which remain the same, but by spiritual experience. This spiritual experience is that of being "enlightened." This enlightenment is not necessarily obvious when it comes to the mind, but finds its expression at a much deeper and more eternal level—the level of awareness, the level of the heart.

This is one reason the Orthodox Church has never withheld baptism from young children. Following the example of the New Testament, young children are included in the members of households who are brought into the Church. In answer to those who ask whether a child is able to understand what is happening to him, most Orthodox would reply that even an adult does not understand what happens when he participates in the Holy Mysteries. Belonging to the Church is not a matter of intellectual choice, but a matter of God gathering His people.

The result of this way of thinking is that children, even babes in arms, are also brought for Holy Communion from the time they are baptized. Children do not hold some sort of second-class position until adolescence, as may be the case in other traditions. On the contrary, when they leave the church building shortly after baptism, they are as much members of the Church, members of the Body of Christ, as the most high-ranking bishop. Once they are enrolled within the Body of Christ, they are, in a very real way, disciples of the Lord, just as St. Matthew's Gospel describes.

St. Paul brings a fascinating dimension to the Church's experience of baptism. He likens the font of baptism to the grave. Thus there are two seemingly unconnected themes in baptism: water and resurrection.

In a sense, water and death represent two aspects of our life, with water, the source of our life as we understand it, contrasting with the waters of drowning. We cannot accept life without accepting the death that is a part of life. Yet the death we receive in baptism is not the terminal sort of physical death, such as we will experience when we leave this present life. Rather, this is a death of transition, in which, independent of our level of awareness, God effects a lasting change in our nature, and we are transformed from one thing into

another—from children of this world into children of the Kingdom
of heaven.

∾: THE BAPTISMAL SERVICE :∾

In Orthodox practice, baptism is performed by triple immersion in
the name of the Holy Trinity. The person baptizing is normally a
priest or a bishop, although there is also a strong tradition that if
someone needs to be baptized in a hurry, anyone is able to perform
this central and most important part of the baptismal service. In such
cases, the person who speaks with ultimate authority on issues such
as these is the bishop of the diocese concerned.

Around the central act of baptism, which only takes a few seconds,
the Church has added a number of other ceremonies, all of which are
designed to heighten our awareness of the significance of the Mystery of Baptism itself. Some of these ceremonies reflect a universal
and eternal experience, while some actually reflect periods of the
Church's life quite different from our own. In the life of the Church
there is a natural reluctance to do away with customs when they
become outdated; rather, new customs are added to them, so that we
sometimes observe different levels of the Church's experience within
very short periods of time. This is a factor that makes Orthodoxy,
with its two thousand years of continuous practice, both fascinating
and complex.

The Catechumenate

For example, some of the traditions concerning baptism reflect the
time when the Church was being savagely persecuted. For most of us
in the modern world, going to church is, at most, somewhat incon-
venient. For members of the persecuted Church, however, going to
church was a matter of life and death—involving both the risk of
imminent physical death and an immediate sense of eternal life—and
attending services was a dangerous and daring thing to do.

If it was dangerous for people to go to church in case hostile eyes
spotted them, it was no less dangerous for the Church to admit

unknown people to its ranks. Certainly, there have been times when being baptized was more than a matter of a few classes and a chat with the priest. During times of persecution, it was important for the members of the Church to be certain that someone applying for baptism was not an agent of the government, planning to infiltrate the Mystical Body in order to carry persecution of the Church to a higher level.

It was possibly for this reason that the early Church evolved a period of preparation for baptism, which gradually became known as the catechumenate. Catechumens were people who were not yet baptized, but who had shown that they were good people, intent on joining the Church. They were given a certain amount of time to prove by their way of life that they were serious about their intentions.

It is for this reason that the modern baptismal service starts with a prayer in which the person to be baptized is admitted to the numbers of the catechumens. In the modern Church, people are generally made catechumens just a few minutes before they are baptized, although in some congregations with large numbers of adults wanting to join the Church, the status of catechumen has been revived.

At various times in the life of the Church, people were expected to remain as catechumens for long periods, months or even years. Indeed, before the Mystery of Confession was fully developed, it was commonly felt that baptism provided a once-and-for-all forgiveness of sins, and that after baptism sin could no longer be forgiven. This belief caused some people to delay baptism until their later years so that they might receive forgiveness towards the end of their life. This practice never reflected the official thinking of the Church, even though it must have been fairly common at times.

Certainly, forgiveness of sins is one of the results of baptism. However, the Orthodox Church has never been overly concerned with the precise nature of the sin being forgiven. The idea of original sin as something inherited from our parents is alien to Orthodox thinking. Here, as elsewhere, the Orthodox Church tends to shy away from speculative theology of any sort, waiting for God to reveal His will and intentions rather than attempting to guess His mind.

The Mystery of Holy Baptism starts in the vestibule just inside the outer western door of the church (assuming the church faces to the east). This is the narthex, the place of the "not-quite," in much the same way that a catechumen is "not quite." It is used for services that do not belong in the place of the fullness of the faith, which is the place where the Divine Liturgy is celebrated.

At the beginning of the service of enrollment among the catechumens, the priest is instructed to breathe three times on the face of the candidate, and three times to make the sign of the cross on the candidate from forehead to breast. This act of breathing in someone's face may seem somewhat odd, but it reminds us that God breathed life into Adam when He created him. The service we are describing will witness the rebirth of the candidate, a rebirth initiated by breath and by the sign of the cross.

The service books state that the candidate for baptism is to be clothed in a single garment, without shoes, and is to face the east. The practice reminds us of the command of God that Moses remove his shoes when he approached the burning bush in the Old Testament story: "This is holy ground." The act of removing shoes for worship in general is still observed by the monks at the Monastery of St. Catherine, the site of the burning bush, but elsewhere in our Church this custom has not been kept. Our brothers and sisters in the Oriental churches (Armenian, Coptic, Syrian, and Ethiopian) would not think of taking part in worship wearing shoes.

Facing east belongs to a far-reaching piece of symbolism that needs some comment. Except in exceptional circumstances, it has always been normal to build Christian churches facing the east. The east is the direction of the rising sun, and since the sun represents light and life, it is quite normal for Christians to turn in that direction for prayer.

Naturally, no one believes that God only lives in the east. If God is God, He is everywhere, and is no more in one direction than another. It is for our own sakes that we arrange churches in such a way as to make the east the focus of our thoughts.

The Exorcisms

Entry into the ranks of the catechumens is preceded by a series of prayers called "exorcisms." Our spiritual ancestors were more likely than we are to see events as the result of intervention by invisible forces of evil, and the baptism service reflects this way of looking at things. The prayers are designed to make the person being baptized aware that there is a certain and definite change going on in his or her life, and that being delivered from the various evil influences and impulses that, realized or not, may have ruled his or her life to that point is an important part of that transformation.

In the last of these prayers, the powers of evil are described in some detail before the various spirits are commanded to leave. The spirits are banished at the word of the priest. It is part of the life of the Church that her priests, like the seventy apostles in the New Testament, are given power over such spirits.

Standing at the door of the church, the priest recites the exorcisms. If any power or presence of evil has any interest whatsoever in the life of the person to be baptized, whether a child or an adult, that evil presence is told to depart.

Facing East, Rejecting Satan, and Turning to Christ

The candidate for baptism, together with the godparents and the priest, turn round to face the west in order to confront, then to defy and reject the powers of darkness. This is done by asking the question, "Do you reject Satan, and all his works, and all his worship and all his angels and all his pomp?" In Orthodox liturgy, many acts and prayers which are regarded as being of supreme importance are recited three times. As may be expected, then, this question is posed three times, and three times comes the answer, "I reject him." As if that were not enough, another question is asked three times: "Have you rejected him?" And again the answer, three times, "I have rejected him."

The decision has been made, the decision has been confirmed, and now the candidate (or, on his or her behalf, the godparent) is asked to seal that decision when the priest says, "Then blow and spit upon him." At this point, the candidate or sponsor takes the remarkably daring step of spitting at the devil. This action contrasts absolutely with the breath of life we saw at the very beginning of the service.

This is a challenge: Spit in the devil's eye! Although this gesture is rarely performed with anything more than polite compliance, at least in modern practice, it is nevertheless a bold thing to do.

The Orthodox Church can never be accused of having any sort of dualist beliefs. In a dualist system there are two sources, one of good and one of evil, and they are locked in an eternal combat with each other, with mankind trapped in the middle. There have been various dualist heresies during the history of the Church, but the Orthodox view has always won the day: the power of God is supreme, and the law of love is all-powerful. In her eternal proclamation, the Church exclaims that the power of the devil, together with the power of death, has already been overthrown through the life-creating events of Christ's life.

It is significant that of all the major services in the Orthodox Church, the Mystery of Holy Baptism is the only occasion on which Satan is mentioned by name or addressed. There is a sense here that just as baptism has a once-for-all quality, so also this rejection of Satan has a lifelong quality. Although the powers of evil continue to try to trick the Christian and to cause her or him to make mistakes, nevertheless the Christian's allegiance is plain. There is no ambivalence in the fact that, no matter the circumstances, he or she is "a child of the light and of the day."

Once this first, challenging part of the service has been completed, the next action is as predictable as it is beautiful. The priest invites the candidate to turn back towards the east, and he or she is asked three times, "Do you turn to Christ?" to which comes the reply each time, "I turn to Christ." Mirroring the set of questions regarding Satan, this question is then repeated, this time in the present tense which makes it mean, "Have you turned to Christ?"

This time, instead of insulting and rejecting (as happened with Satan), the candidate is invited to submit to God, to bow down and worship. This brings to mind the occasion when Satan invited Jesus to fall down and worship him. Jesus refused to do so, saying of God, "Only Him will you serve." Thus, by action and by taking the words of Jesus literally, the candidate for baptism now bows down before God the Holy Trinity, accepting Him as his King and his God.

As if in a state of relief, the priest leads the candidate towards the font, saying, "Blessed is God, who wills that all men should be saved and come to the knowledge of the truth, always, now and forever and to the ages of ages." Once they arrive, the priest prays a final prayer, and the preliminary service comes to a close.

The Baptism Proper

The candidate is not yet technically a catechumen; that actually happens shortly before immersion. However, everything is now ready, and the baptism itself can start. At this point, particularly if the candidate is a baby, the godparents (and the parents if necessary) prepare the baby, undressing him and wrapping him in a towel or some other clothing that can easily be removed. Meanwhile, because the celebration of baptism is not only an important social event, but also one of the central Holy Mysteries in the life of the Church, the priest puts on his outer vestment, called a *phelonion*. Incense is blessed, and the whole atmosphere of the event becomes filled with anticipation that something important is about to happen.

The event starts with the proclamation that begins the important public prayers of the Church: "Blessed is the Kingdom of the Father and of the Son and of the Holy Spirit, now and forever, and to the ages of ages, amen."

The priest makes the sign of the cross over the place of baptism with the Book of the Gospels, just as he does at the beginning of the Divine Liturgy over the altar table. The font or the body of water to be used for baptism therefore takes on some of the characteristics of the holy altar, not only as a place where God is present, but also as a place where an offering is to be made. This ability to join two concepts like this with a single symbolic gesture is part of the genius of Orthodox liturgy.

The Service of Holy Baptism starts with the blessing of the water. Water is treated with great respect in the Church, particularly water that has been set aside with a special blessing. The form of blessing used in the baptismal service is much the same as that used on January 5 and 6, when the Baptism of our Lord is commemorated. The words used in this blessing are ancient and beautiful, in loose poetry where ideas echo each other as they hymn the relationship between God and His creation. The prayer comes to a climax when God is asked to sanctify the water by His presence. This presence is almost always described in a Trinitarian form in Orthodox prayers. This is particularly significant in the Mystery of Baptism, since it was at the baptism of Jesus that the Holy Trinity was first shown to the world.

An element of exorcism is present in this prayer also, just in case any presence of evil should be "hiding and lurking" in the water. This touches a chord in the imagination of many people, since we inherited from our ancestors a fear of water; certainly, if water can bring blessing, it can also bring trouble. The prayer includes a reminder of the power of the Cross to defeat "all adverse powers," and the priest outlines the form of the cross three times in the body of the water with his hand.

The next prayer is the blessing of the oil that will mark the candidate for baptism as a catechumen. At the beginning of the service, this is simply ordinary olive oil, which can be bought at any grocery store and is customarily brought to the church by the godparent. This oil is blessed by the priest performing the baptism, and from that moment it loses its ordinary status and is set aside for special uses. The priest breathes on the oil three times and makes the sign of the cross over it three times, just as he did at the very beginning of the service over the baptismal candidate. The priest asks that the oil might be blessed through the work of the Holy Spirit, and that it might become "an anointing for incorruption, an armor of righteousness, a renewal of soul and body, for an aversion of every assault of the devil, and a deliverance from evil of all who are anointed with it, or who partake of it."

Having blessed the oil, the priest pours it three times in the form of a cross upon the baptismal water. Pouring oil upon water is a complex and beautiful symbol, usually associated with the bringing of peace. The candidate is then anointed on several parts of his body, with appropriate verses from Scripture spoken at each anointing.

In some parts of the Orthodox Church, the godparent now completes the task begun by the priest. First, he receives the oil in his cupped hands, which he holds over the font. Then, once the priest has been given the child to hold, the godparent covers the baby with the oil. This practice may not be of the most ancient origin, but it is certainly the high point of the ministry of the godparent. In Greek speech, the godparent is described as the one who baptizes the child, not the priest—although in fact it is the task of the godparent to anoint with the oil of the catechumens, not to perform the baptism proper. However, since the baptism itself is the next action to occur, this is perhaps an understandable exaggeration.

The baptism itself is a brief and moving ceremony. The child is placed in the water three times, and the wording is pronounced, "The servant of God N. is baptized in the name of the Father and of the Son and of the Holy Spirit." This is the central action everyone present has come to witness. Just as a newborn child is washed shortly after birth, so this washing accompanies the child's rebirth—his being born again, not now into time, which comes with its own demise, but into life, which is, in quality, eternal.

This is what we mean when we say that baptism leaves an indelible mark, a mark God alone can see. It gives the person an eternal dimension, and it happens right there in the font. Eternal life is not a human condition by right, only by grace. The action of the Holy Spirit gives this divine quality to the candidate, so that rising from the water he now "lives unto God," as we will hear later in the epistle reading. Christ died for sin, once and for all, so that we might rise to a new life in Him for all eternity. The baptized person is buried and resurrected in the water. He dies to sin and lives to God.

The Chrismation

After the baptism, events tend to move quickly. This is largely because the newly baptized infant is often crying by this point. In order to make the experience as easy as possible, it is customary, at least in the Greek Church, to perform all the actions together, leaving the prayers for the time when the baby is being clothed. Although the actions may take place quickly, they are nevertheless very significant.

The next thing that happens, the chrismation, is so important that it is regarded as a separate Mystery altogether. In the practice of the Orthodox Church, it is performed separately only in the case of someone who, according to the canons and rules of the Church, is received into the Church by chrismation rather than by baptism. Chapter 9, which examines chrismation, will take up that subject more fully.

Unlike the oil of the catechumens, which begins the service as ordinary oil and is then blessed by the priest, the oil used at the time of chrismation is far from ordinary. It has already been blessed, not by the priest, nor even by the bishop of the diocese. This oil is generally blessed by a patriarch, or the head of an independent Church, and then only on fairly rare occasions. Once blessed, this oil, which is mixed with a number of other ingredients, is called myrrh or chrism. It is sent out through the archbishops and metropolitans to all the parishes in communion with the patriarch who blessed the oil. Chrism is used not only on people. It is also used in the consecration of a church and, in some ancient traditions, the blessing of icons.

Chrism is treated with great respect, and only small amounts are generally used. The neophyte is anointed as he was with the oil of the catechumens a few minutes earlier, and at each anointing the priest says the words, "The seal of the gift of the Holy Spirit."

The Holy Spirit is, in Orthodox experience, the agent of each and every Mystery. In chrismation the action of the Holy Spirit is seen as sealing the act of baptism, much as the decisions of the candidate to repudiate Satan, then to accept Christ, were sealed before baptism with the symbolic actions of spitting in one direction, then bowing in worship in the other. The word "seal" implies something that keeps something else intact: the seal on a letter, the seal on a bottle of expensive wine or perfume. The water of baptism will dry up, but the action of the Holy Spirit seals the action of baptism for all time.

The more obvious symbolism, imitating the words of the Gospel, that man is born again through water and the Spirit is thus acted out with great clarity.

In the light of this practice, it is perhaps unnecessary to think of baptism and chrismation as two separate Mysteries. In many ways, not least liturgically, they are simply parts of one and the same Sacrament.

The Tonsure and Clothing

In practice, a few more ceremonies now follow in quick succession: the cutting of hair (called the "tonsure"), the giving of a white garment, and, although it is not usually mentioned in the service books, the giving of a cross. Each of these actions requires some comment.

The cutting of hair, in the form of a cross, is so far removed from our daily lives that it is not at all obvious why it is done. This is particularly true in the case of a baby who has almost no hair. Certainly, as a priest, I sometimes feel uncomfortable to be presented with a child who is still wet and oily, possibly struggling, only to find that there is no hair to cut.

There are, in fact, three tonsures in the life of the Church. This is the first, and the only one that is performed on every member of the Church. Authorities vary on the exact meaning of this ceremony. However, the one I find most enlightening involves the history of slavery.

Happily, slavery in its traditional sense is almost unknown in the modern world. But even in America, a country built on a foundation of equality, slavery is only about a hundred and fifty years distant from us today.

In a society in which slavery was common, there were many different ways of showing that someone was a slave and not a free person. Shackles of some sort, or a uniform, might be acceptable in some societies, but one fairly common method of designating a slave was to shave off all his or her hair. In many cultures, this not only had the function of indicating who was a slave and who was not, but it was also a mark of dishonor. Having one's hair cut against one's own wishes constitutes a significant affront to one's sense of personhood.

However, when we do this in church, even symbolically, there is another layer of experience. Baptism marks a transition from old ways to new, from death to life, from the ways of this world to the ways of the Kingdom. In one sense, the candidate for baptism is exchanging enslavement to this world for enslavement to God.

It is worth bearing in mind that from the moment of baptism onwards, whenever that person comes to the church for anything official or significant, he will be given the title "the slave of God" followed by his baptismal name. This is the case when he comes for Holy Communion, to be married, to be anointed, and, eventually, when he is carried into church for the last time. Far from being a cause for shame, the title "slave of God" is one we should carry with great pride, since it is in being a slave of God that we enjoy perfect freedom.

Next the candidate is given a white garment to wear. The newly baptized is dressed, just as the Church herself wears a special dress at Easter during the time called Bright Week. According to the service books, although this is no longer a common practice, the newly baptized is ordered to return to church a week after the baptism in order for the white baptismal garment to be removed. The practicality of having an adult wear a white garment continuously for a week must always have been a problem, and for an infant even more so. However, the Church retains the custom of giving the garment immediately after baptism, and the prayer for its removal eight days later. This is combined with a symbolic removal of the oils of baptism and chrismation.

The giving of the cross is a gesture that requires little comment, unless we need to point out the significance of wearing a cross at all. In general, Orthodox Christians wear a cross around their necks at all times. Thus, it is appropriate that a person being baptized should be given a cross at the baptism, usually as a gift from the godparent. In some situations, wearing the cross may mean little. In a situation that is actively hostile to religious belief in general or to Christianity in particular, more than a little courage may be needed to wear it.

The rite of baptism is concluded with a joyful, though sedate, dance around the font, followed by readings from Scripture. In the Gospel we actually hear the words of Jesus Himself.

Prayers for the neophyte, the newly enlightened slave of God, follow, together with prayers for his or her godparents and parents and for all those who have come together to celebrate this Holy Mystery. The dismissal follows, and the party then generally moves on to celebrations of a more secular nature.

In reality, the Mystery of Initiation is not yet complete. This will only happen when the neophyte is brought back to the church during the Divine Liturgy in order to receive Holy Communion.

~: CHAPTER 9 :~

The Mystery of Chrismation

THE PRAYERS OF THE CHRISMATION SERVICE SPEAK OF grace—the grace of the gift of the Holy Spirit—as a reminder that when we enter into the life of God through baptism and chrismation, we are totally and obviously on the receiving end of God's love. All we need to do is to be present. God promises to do all the rest. No one can be naturally worthy of baptism or chrismation—it is a free gift, and the only possible authentic response is grateful acceptance.

~: MARKED FOR THE KINGDOM :~

One of the strongest pieces of symbolism associated with chrismation is that we are thereby marked for the Kingdom.

Being a "marked person" is a powerful biblical image, from the days of Cain and Abel right up to the Book of Revelation, in which the world is divided, in typical apocalyptic fashion, into the obviously good and the obviously evil. Those marked with the sign of evil are on one side, while those washed clean in the blood of the Lamb are on the other.

Markings are made so that people and objects can be known. In the case of Cain, the purpose of the mark was to let people know that they were not to harm him. His therapy was to stay alive, not to lose himself in the oblivion of death at the hands of those who wanted to avenge the death of Abel. This story, so often misunderstood, underlines the fact that the spiritual path is open to everyone at any time, no matter how bad they are or how bad they think they are—even to someone who blatantly and sickeningly kills his own innocent brother. However, on the path there is work to be done.

The sign bestowed in chrismation is itself invisible, just like the qualities to which it gives birth. It is made visible by outward indications, such as the cross and the white garment. But it is the invisible reality that is important.

This invisible reality exists on two levels. The first level is that in chrismation, we are marked as belonging—we are given an eternal sense of belonging to the Body of Christ. This mark cannot be rubbed off, no matter how badly we perform, and no matter what struggles are going on inside us and around us. We are marked for God, and we are marked for life.

Belonging is described in the Orthodox Church in terms of "being in communion." This means far more than that two particular people can receive Holy Communion together. It is, rather, a declaration of being "in Christ," that fundamental awareness of identity, of participating in the life of the Church and the life of God. To be "in communion" is the primary sense of being within the Church. It is far more significant than one's specific role or position within the Church. Everyone, from the patriarch to the youngest baptized person, is "in communion" and thus "in Christ"—a status which is both egalitarian and remarkable.

St. Paul, in the epistle read during the Mystery of Baptism, talks of "putting off" the old man (essentially our identity as a citizen of this world) and putting on the new (our identity as members of the Body of Christ and children and inheritors of the Kingdom). However, in another place, St. Peter uses exactly the same theme when he talks about putting off the body of the old man in death (2 Peter 1:14). This gives us a clear indication not only that leaving one state of life and adopting another is like death, but also that in death there is no loss of being "in communion." Death is merely a transition from one level of communion to another.

Thus the sense of belonging, an adoption of an essential identity, is paramount in the way in which the Orthodox Church sees herself.

This provides the human personality with great comfort in a world often seen to be hostile, projecting a clear sense of alienation. The gift of the Holy Spirit, the dynamic spiritual movement, gives the person a sense of belonging that the world is unable to eradicate. Through the Holy Spirit, the individual puts on the armor of light and thus is changed. His or her potential is magnified beyond measure, because the person now has the ability to grow towards deeper and yet deeper participation in the life of God. For that person, the sky is no longer the limit.

The second aspect of the mark bestowed in chrismation, also invisible, is that we become inheritors of the gifts of the Spirit. Within the life of God—within the Holy Trinity, but also in our own participation in the life of God through baptism and chrismation—the regular rules of life are completely altered. In place of fear and greed, we are presented with generosity and confidence. In place of insecurity and alienation, we are firmly given a sense of belonging and identity.

The theme of "sealing" is another of particular significance. Recalling the experience of the persecuted Church in the days of the Apocalypse of St. John, the sense of being marked is deepened into a sense of being sealed. Sealing something is not a common practice in the modern world, unless you count sealing an envelope by licking the flap. In days of old, a letter would be sealed with wax and a seal—a special object bearing a unique design, which would enable the letter to be identified by anyone capable of deciphering it. Seals bore a sense of guarantee that what was sealed was important and special in some way, as well as more hidden significance for those who knew how to interpret the seal.

Sealing makes something special. When we are sealed in chrismation, we become special—the one thing that in our fallen mental condition we all crave. However (and this is not what the mind wants to hear), God has the ability to make us aware that we are special, but without diminishing the "special" quality of everyone else. God is capable of placing everyone simultaneously on center stage.

In Galatians 5:22–23, St. Paul lists the qualities one might expect to be natural and normal within our experience of God: love, joy, peace, longsuffering, kindness, goodness, faithfulness, gentleness, self-control. These qualities are not normal in the outside world; sometimes they are not even apparent. But life in Christ is not like life in this world. Almost always, it is in contrast.

Our own life within the Church does not always reflect these qualities of the Kingdom. Yet they are normative, in the sense of belonging intrinsically to our participation in the life of God. The fact that we do not always notice the life of God reflected obviously in the life of the Church does not make this statement any less true. When the Church is being Church, particularly when it is assembled around the altar, it is nothing less than a reflection of the life of the Holy Trinity, in which the common currency is love and the common time-frame eternity.

This exceptional and beautiful environment can, unfortunately, be defeated by the will of man, as can almost any action of God. Naturally, the whole Church never loses its obvious identity, but this identity may, like most of the actions of the Holy Spirit, be hidden rather deeply. Nevertheless, just as the formal life of the Church exists when she celebrates the liturgy, so the most obvious life of God exists also at that time. Few are those who are able to behave in a parish council meeting as they do in the Divine Liturgy.

~: ONE MYSTERY IN TWO :~

To divide baptism and chrismation into two separate Mysteries is, in most conditions, both unnecessary and confusing. Baptism is, in a sense, the preparation for chrismation, while chrismation is equally the completion of baptism. To place the two in separate boxes is to misunderstand their interdependence. It is only in certain cases that these Mysteries are celebrated separately, and then always when the Church is showing particular care and concern for individuals whose situation is anomalous.

The relationship between the Mystery of Chrismation and the Mystery of Baptism is that of a visa compared with a passport. We receive the passport in baptism, but it is made usable and workable in chrismation. The visa does not change nationality, but it gives a new dimension of action, opens a new range of possibility. Chrismation brings the work of God to fullness and completes the identity of the individual who receives it.

For those who join the Orthodox Church through chrismation, its significance is different from the normal experience of receiving baptism and chrismation together. What happens in this case is that the untold benevolence of God is used to make right something that is not quite right. From the view of the Orthodox Church, a person received through the Mystery of Chrismation has everything about him or her put right in the eyes of the Church. A baptism performed outside the Orthodox Church is thus made Orthodox by the Mystery of Chrismation and, in some parts of the Orthodox Church, this is thought to be true of any marriage performed outside the Orthodox Church as well.

Under the circumstances prevailing in the modern world, in which those who come from other Christian traditions enter the Orthodox Church through Holy Chrismation, as well as in situations outlined in the canons for those who return to the Orthodox Church after apostasy, this Mystery is itself the door to salvation.

My own chrismation as a convert from the Anglican Church still provides me with a very clear memory. Celebrated on the afternoon of Lazarus Saturday, just before Vespers, it enabled me to take part fully in the life of the Church during Great and Holy Week. According to the custom, I had made an appointment to spend some time with the priest before the service started, and at that point had made a general confession. On that occasion I was still not "in communion" with the Body of Christ, and thus I had to wait a few hours before receiving the forgiveness which is the common currency of life in the Church. Indeed, at the point at which I did receive forgiveness for the first time as an Orthodox, I was still not actually a member of the Church. But in such situations there is a deep spiritual anticipation, and participation in the Mystery actually reshapes the fabric of time.

For the convert received through the Mystery of Chrismation (which is the practice of the Ecumenical Patriarchate), there is a special sense of returning home that accompanies this service. Not so much a rejection of one Christian community in favor of another, it is much more the act of coming home of the estranged son. The destiny was home all the time, but that fact had not been realized.

The act of coming home is in itself an icon of the spiritual life. The source of all life is God. That in itself is no miracle; that is just how it is. Returning to the source, however, does have a miraculous quality. Once the ingredient of freedom has been introduced, without which love itself is impotent, there is an unknown element and inevitability is lost. In the court of heaven, the return of the lost sheep is always awaited, but that does not make that return inevitable.

The moment of chrismation marks a significant step in that journey home.

~: CHAPTER 10 :~

Divine Liturgy &
Holy Communion

AT THE VERY HEART OF THE PRACTICE OF THE CHRIS-
tian faith is the act of participation in the offering of bread and wine.
A simple response of the Church to the commandment, "Do this in
remembrance of Me" (Luke 22:19), the Divine Liturgy is the time
when the Church really is the Church in a way it is not at other times.
The Divine Liturgy is eternity in time, and for those who take part, it
is the experience of the Kingdom which both is and is to come.

The Divine Liturgy is the source of strength *par excellence* of the
person trying to follow the commands and precepts of the Gospel.
It is joy, consolation, encouragement, and instruction. It is commitment—not only our commitment to God, but also God's commitment to us. In its celebration, heaven and earth blend into each other,
and God touches His Church, both at a corporate level—the Body of
Christ standing in the body of the church, meeting with and participating in the Body of Christ in the holy chalice—and at an individual
level: the people approach the holy chalice one by one to experience a
deeply personal encounter with the King of the universe.

When the members of a community meet together for the Divine
Liturgy, particularly on a Sunday morning, they enter into an eternal
ambience, one in which the time and geography of the world are of little importance. At the proclamation, "Blessed is the Kingdom of the

Father and of the Son and of the Holy Spirit, now and for ever and to the ages of ages," the Church—the people, the building, even the concept of "church"—is transfigured and becomes itself an expression of the Kingdom. Icons are protrusions of the Kingdom into our dimension, but after the proclamation of the Kingdom (which is the work of the Gospel), the Church—people and building—surpasses the role of icons. Icons are material and lifeless. The Church at the liturgy is the living expression of the presence of God in His world.

Naturally, within the church building the rules of physics still apply, since it is not in God's nature to compromise or disturb the means by which He governs the universe. However, at some spiritual level it is true that if someone leaves behind the outside world and pushes open the door of the church building where the Church is gathered for the Divine Liturgy, that person is entering another time and space, or indeed (and perhaps more correctly) all time and all space. In eternal life, every moment is now and everywhere is here. Thus the distances of time and space that normally divide us—say, from the earthly ministry of our Lord two thousand years ago—are here of no importance. This division still exists outside the church building; however, within the church, the Kingdom is present, and all time and all places are right here and right now.

At the beginning of each celebration of the Holy Mysteries, the priest proclaims, "Blessed is the Kingdom of the Father and of the Son and of the Holy Spirit." This is sometimes interpreted as a statement of declaration: that the Kingdom of heaven is the goal and the aim of our participation in the holy services. This is certainly true. However, this statement has another significance.

In the original Greek text, or indeed in the Slavonic translation, there is no word for "is." The priest actually says, "Blessed the Kingdom . . ." There is no verb, and more importantly there is no tense. It is "is," but it is also "was" and "will be"—it is the eternal now, the "acceptable time" of which St. Paul speaks (2 Corinthians 6:2). It is as if the action of starting the service captures eternity. Certainly, for all who take part in the Holy Mystery, for the duration of the service an element of eternity projects into time, leaving an indelible mark. The person who receives the Mystery of the Bread and Wine encounters

God, and in that meeting he or she is changed, because any meeting with God involves both judgment and change. Even if not immediately apparent, that change has eternal consequences.

When the Divine Liturgy begins, all the members of the family of God, of every age and of every place, are naturally present. The heavenly court is there, of course, and will take an active part in the service itself. All the saints and friends of God of every age are also present, participating in whatever way they may. Sometimes the priest or the deacon may be seen swinging the incense-burner and bowing towards a part of the building that appears to be empty. In reality, of course, within the Kingdom, nothing is empty, everything is presence; there is no place where the Presence is not. To attend and participate in the Divine Liturgy is to be present in the Presence in a way that is not normally possible for human beings.

The members of the community worshipping at the Divine Liturgy are already participating in the Kingdom. They are already the perfection they are seeking to achieve. This does not necessarily mean that they will feel anything, or think anything in particular, and it is certainly not a matter for self-congratulation, since it is entirely the work of God that allows this miracle to happen. We make an offering which is far from perfect when it leaves our hands, but by the time our offering is accepted and returned to us in the form of Holy Communion, it has been made perfect. The offering community is itself transformed and transfigured, just like the bread and wine.

The offering that takes place at the Divine Liturgy has a subtle, parallel significance. The theme of "the Body of Christ" is echoed back and forth between the body of Christians standing in the church, on the one hand, and the bread and wine lying on the holy table on the other. Even at the high point, the *epiclesis*, when God the Holy Spirit is invited to make the transformation of the bread and wine complete, the prayer of the Church is that the Holy Spirit will also come "upon us." Our transformation is at once as symbolic and as real as is the transformation of the bread and wine into the Body and the Blood. Certainly, the transformation of the bread and wine is a process, not a single point of time, just as the transformation of the people is gradual. However, people can and do change in ways mere bread and wine do not. The potential for change in people is much greater. Even so, the bread and wine are transformed in an ultimate way: they enter the Kingdom not as mere food (which would be important enough), but as the presence of God Himself. How much greater, then, is the potential for transformation of the people of God?

❂ THE SERVICE OF THE DIVINE LITURGY ❧

The initial offering of the bread and wine generally takes place before the people arrive for the liturgy. This offering and the initial prayers—the great litany together with the psalms that used to be sung in full and the small litanies that came between them—all these prayers were once said in another place, away from the place of the liturgy. The Church then moved as a body into the church (around the holy table): "Come let us worship and fall down before Christ."

This piece of ceremony, now obvious only when a bishop celebrates the Divine Liturgy, shines like a flashlight back in time to the days of persecution, of secret gatherings, when membership in the Church meant a commitment not only of one's time and efforts, but possibly of one's life as well. The theme of martyrdom is never far from the worshiping Church, since fragments of the bones of the saints are enshrined in the holy table and often in the *antimension* (the holy tablecloth) as well. Nor does the torch have to shine back very far in order to find examples of this level of Christian commitment in relatively modern times.

The Liturgy of the Word

The hymn "Holy God" and the prayers that surround it are a very potent message to the worshipping community. This hymn began, in rather inglorious fashion, as simply a verse recited before certain scriptures. Over the centuries, however, it has been elevated to its present importance and dimension. It affords one of the rare occasions when the priest (speaking, as he almost always does, for the whole worshipping community) stands at the altar and has the audacity to tell God that He is "holy." This statement, so obvious, so potent, challenges and defeats all and every power wishing to disrupt the relationship between God and His Church. We acknowledge God as holy, we acknowledge God as strong, we acknowledge God as immortal—and the only possible topping of this statement, the only possible response to the greatness of God, is to plead for mercy.

At the reading of the epistle, we catch a glimpse of a definitive icon of the Church in listening mode. Here we remember that there must be times when the entire Church listens to the voice of God. The bishop sits in his throne behind the holy table, facing the people. To each side sit his clergy. The people stand or sit listening to the words of the apostle, read outside the altar area.

The Gospel, by contrast, is proclaimed, and no one sits during its reading. Since the Gospel reading describes the life and work of the Lord and often contains the very words He spoke, the listening of the Church must rise to a higher level. It is in these words that the Church finds the very reason for her existence.

After the Gospel and the sermon, whose major task is to proclaim the words of the Gospel, the major prayers of intercession take place. Unfortunately, in some churches, these prayers are often omitted, distorting the clear shape of the ancient liturgy. This leaves the great litany at the beginning of the service to fulfill this important function, a task for which it is not really suited.

Unfortunate, too, is the omission of the prayers for the catechumens which follow immediately upon the completion of the intercessory prayers. Although there may be few in the ranks of the catechumens in many parishes, these prayers (together with the dismissal, "Catechumens depart, let no catechumen remain") are a vivid reminder to church members that they, by virtue of their baptism, now stand as members of the elect, the remnant called out from the rest of the world, the Church in its fullness, the *ekklesia*.

The Liturgy of the Gifts

The great entrance, when the bread and wine are carried to the holy table in procession, is at its heart simply the presentation of the offerings of the people. Just as the tiny pieces of bread on the holy plate, carried by the deacon or priest, represent individual members of the Body of Christ present in the body of the church, so the people standing in church represent the offering to God. The link between the people and the offering of bread and wine—the basic food groups of our spiritual ancestors—is very powerful, just as the deep identity between the Person of Christ and the Body of Christ is extraordinarily profound.

During the great entrance the choir sings, "Let us put aside all the cares of this life, that we may receive the King of all, invisibly surrounded by the ranks of angels." This is no small matter. Putting aside the cares of this life is one of the most important, yet one of the most difficult, things a human being can do. The hymn instructs us to get out of our minds and into our hearts. We spend almost all our lives in our minds, worrying about what has happened in the past and worrying about what might happen in the future. In order to meet God, we have to put both these activities aside and concentrate on the present moment, since it is there that we meet God. To do this, we need to put aside our minds (they will be ready and waiting for us later) and enter the profound silence of our hearts.

Just before the offerings are placed on the altar, Jesus Himself is addressed as the "One who offers and the One who is offered." This beautiful summary of the theology of the Church highlights the spiritual complexity of the relatively simple act of offering bread and wine.

Slowly, because the Church wants to treasure these sacred moments, the liturgy reaches its climax. The life of Christ is memorialized, the words of the Last Supper proclaimed. Then the entire Church waits for the Holy Spirit to intervene and to complete the offering, and thus complete the transformation. During this time, various Christian virtues are highlighted. One such connection, not necessarily an obvious one in the eyes of the world, is that between love and faith.

Just before the recitation of the creed, the statement of the faith of the Holy Orthodox Church, the priest calls on the congregation to love one another. The idea of the Church as a congregation of love is not simply a pretty thought; it is an absolute necessity for the expression of the faith. Any amount of right doctrine is of no importance at all if it is not shared in love. We need to be constantly reminded in this way that faith depends on love, not on a worldly desire to be right. Nowhere does Jesus command His disciples to be "right." Rather, He commands them to be "righteous." This applies with equal force to us as it did to His first disciples two thousand years ago. We cannot offer faith to God, since faith is and can only be a gift from God to us. We can, however, offer love. We thus get to offer what we can, not what we cannot.

The exact wording of this invitation is very revealing. The words, rightfully belonging to the deacon, whose job it is to instruct the congregation about what they need to do, command (not just commend!) the congregation to love one another, that with oneness of nous (*omonoia*) they may speak out loud a summary of faith whose meaning can only be heard when it emerges from love. Achieving oneness of mind is probably not possible in a fallen world. Achieving oneness of heart is.

A second living icon of the Church to which special attention should be given is what takes place at the raising up of the bread and wine. The identity between the bread and the wine and the Body and Blood of Christ is now almost complete. The Church has recalled the words of Jesus at the Last Supper, and has recollected the other life-creating events in the life, death, and resurrection of the Lord. Now the bishop or priest stands back and allows the deacon to raise the bread and wine, the dish and the cup, while the words *"Ta sa ek ton son si prosferomen, kata panta kai dia panta"* are sung.

These words are so full of meaning in the original Greek text that to replace them with those of another language could take a long time. The words mean something like this: "We offer You these gifts, which are, in reality, part of those gifts You have already given to us, and we do so in a way that makes them represent all the needs and desires, all the hopes and thoughts, all the weaknesses and shortcomings of all of us and of all mankind."

The place of the deacon in this living icon is noteworthy. At this most sacred moment, the bishop takes a step back, although he remains the source of authority within the local church. The bread and wine are actually held by the deacon, who has that distinct role in the Church—not quite a priest, not quite a layman, but in some sense both. He, uniquely, presents the gifts on behalf of the whole Church.

The prayer to the Holy Spirit that follows immediately seals the offering of the bread and wine, much as the Holy Spirit seals the act of baptism in the Mystery of Christian initiation. The Holy Trinity is now both present and made manifest in the life and experience of the Church in the world.

Holy Communion

Holy Communion, the supreme act of the Church and perhaps the most significant living icon presented to us by the Divine Liturgy, is both the climax of the service and the climax of the lives of those who are taking part in it. In the Divine Liturgy, the whole of the action builds up to the point of Communion. However, that point depends not on our emotional condition, and even less on our level of understanding, since there is nothing to understand. What takes place is a meeting—an encounter. It takes place at God's invitation and by God's grace.

The preparation we are encouraged to make before receiving Holy Communion has as its main aim the realization of our unworthiness. There is nothing we can do to make ourselves worthy of receiving Holy Communion. On the contrary, we always (in the words of St. Paul) eat and drink to our condemnation. It is the love of God and His desire to be close to His people that allows us to walk away from the experience unharmed.

The fast before Communion has its roots in a desire to give honor to God. All too often, though, it feels like some sort of punishment. Indeed, in our culture, there may be many times when we feel fasting of any kind is a punishment. Here is an area where a swift attitude adjustment is needed. A good and more positive understanding of the Communion fast is that from the moment we wake up, we should be aware of our longing for God. Not having breakfast is a part of that longing. We learn to look forward to the moment of receiving Holy

Communion, not rejecting the time that lies in between, but savoring each moment.

There has long been a tendency to create a division between the act of the worshipping Church in the Divine Liturgy and the act of the individual worshipper in receiving Holy Communion. This is unique among the Holy Mysteries. The act of baptism is never seen as something separate from the service of baptism, nor the crowning in weddings, nor the central act in any other Mystery.

The difficulty seems to lie in the fact that for many members of the Orthodox Church, attendance at the Divine Liturgy is a frequent occurrence, whereas taking part in Holy Communion is not. Indeed, there may be good reasons why people are encouraged to receive Holy Communion only infrequently, and then only after intense preparation, including fasting and the Mystery of Confession. I remember listening to a senior bishop, someone I admire very much, saying that he was happy to be able to attend a Sunday liturgy from time to time when he was not the celebrant, since this meant that, for him, Holy Communion was not an automatic, frequent event. However, since he was a bishop, it was normal for him to serve the Divine Mysteries each time he attended, which meant that he received Holy Communion every Sunday.

I can understand why he felt as he did. It is so easy to allow the reception of Holy Communion to be something merely routine, rather than ensuring that it is the high point of the week. Almost from the beginning of its history, there has been a tension in the Church between the need to receive Holy Communion frequently and the need to receive it with care.

In receiving Holy Communion, a number of things happen. Certainly we meet God in a very direct, not to say intimate, fashion. It would be difficult to imagine a more intimate contact, and certainly the act of Holy Communion outshines any human attempt at intimacy a thousand times over. We also receive nourishment, not for our bodily needs (although it is real food) but for our spiritual needs: "for forgiveness of sins and for eternal life." This eternal life is not something that will start in some distant future, but something which is a reality at this moment.

There is a monastic tradition, whose written source I have never found, that it is a good thing to spend a great deal of time and effort preparing for a meal, then to spend as little time and effort as possible eating it. It looks like one of those traditions that challenges the normal course of human behavior in favor of pointing to something higher.

Certainly, having received Holy Communion at the Divine Liturgy, the Church shows no inclination to wait around, as diners might sit around a table at the end of a meal. In fact, having experienced this spiritual singularity, the Church immediately continues on her mission, sensing her identity as the herald of the Kingdom. Having been touched by God, we go out into the world to proclaim the Kingdom to all nations—not with our words or actions, but by who we are, or more correctly, who we have become through the actions of the Holy Spirit. The dismissal at the Divine Liturgy is not the beginning of the end, but merely the end of the beginning.

❦ THE DIVINE LITURGY AND SILENCE ❧

As a general rule, we can say that there is silence at the heart of our experience of God (*hesychia*). Strangely, in the Divine Liturgy, there is a complete lack of physical silence. Often, the chanter or the choir feels compelled to fill silence with noise of some sort. This has been the case for a long time, as we can see from the common Byzantine practice of adding nonsense syllables (*te-re-re* or *ne-ne-ne*) to hymns which need to cover a particular ceremonial action by the clergy and their assistants.

There is silence in the Divine Liturgy, however. That silence is to be found in the hearts of the worshippers. Physical silence sometimes encourages us to go off into dreamland or fantasy, and that is the last thing we need to do in the Divine Liturgy. We cannot, after all, meet God in imagination or fantasy, and the hymns encourage us to stay focused on our awareness of being in the Presence. Silence is the language of God, and it is in silence, the deep silence of the heart, that we both listen and speak.

~: CHAPTER II :~

The Mystery of Confession & Forgiveness

THE ACT OF HOLY COMMUNION LIES AT THE CENTER OF our sense of belonging to Christ. As a group, we enjoy the deepest intimacy when the Body of Christ is nourished with the Body and Blood of Christ.

If Holy Communion is at the center of this life-giving experience, the Mystery of Confession finds us at the outermost layers of our Christian life. Here we, as individuals, stand as outsiders seeking admittance, or rather readmittance, into the Kingdom of heaven.

Confession might well be called the Mystery of Forgiveness, since forgiveness is not natural in this world and remains a mystery, no matter how familiar we are with it. It only makes real sense in terms of eternal life and the ways of the Kingdom. In this, as in every other Mystery of the Church, we see the Kingdom emerging into our fallen dimension. This is yet another example of the protrusion of God's eternity into our time.

Underlying the entire experience of confession, we need to be aware that forgiveness, whether by God or by another human being, does not make sense. Indeed, according to the thinking of this world, it is nonsense. We are told from early in our lives that you never get something for nothing, everything has to be earned and paid for, and there is no such thing as a free lunch. Yet that is exactly what forgiveness is.

It is a completely free gift. All we have to do is ask for it. However, we do have to ask for it—it is not delivered to us automatically.

Furthermore, the forgiveness received in the Church is unlike a pardon that might be received in a secular situation. In the world, forgiveness involves having the slate wiped clean; but the guilt remains, since forgiveness is given by an act of will. In confession, the forgiveness we receive is nothing less than an act of love. It not only wipes out the badness of what is forgiven, but also (to use the expression in the form of the Lord's Prayer we use in the Church) forgives what is "owed."

One of the most important features of the Mystery of Forgiveness is that it allows the individual to start again with a clean slate. This allows us to get rid of the detritus of the mind—all those thoughts and feelings that drag us down.

~: THE CONTEXT OF CONFESSION :~

It is probably not too much of an exaggeration to say that confession is the Mystery which overlaps most frequently with the work of healers in the secular world. Although confession exists in an entirely spiritual context, it has enough overlap with psychotherapy to make a comparison worthwhile. One area in which confession and therapy have an obvious connection is that both require a safe space in order to be effective, and it is the patient, or the one making confession, who decides whether there is safety or not. This safety is shown in two ways in particular.

First, the place of therapy—a corner of the church, a special room, or even an office or a space in a private house—has to be such that the person feels safe in terms of secrecy and confidentiality. A great deal of what is most important in confession is the disclosure of things that are the source of shame. By definition, things that carry shame are difficult to talk about, and a special, safe place is necessary if much progress is to be made.

Secondly, just like the patient with his therapist, the penitent has to have confidence in the priest who leads him or her towards the Mystery of Forgiveness. Confidentiality around this Mystery must be absolute for the penitent to feel secure and to talk openly.

The penitent must also feel secure that no matter what he or she says, the minister of the Mystery will not react in a shocked or abrupt manner. The Orthodox priest is not present to judge the penitent, but rather to be a witness. God is the judge, and God desires the repentance, the inner transformation, of the one who has gone astray. A penitent who has been shamed by parental figures in the past will not react at all well if the minister of this Holy Mystery does the same thing.

Everything disclosed must be greeted by the priest with empathy, and above all with his presence. The priest, as the minister of the Mystery, has the very difficult task of staying completely present throughout the time the penitent is talking. Some of the greatest confessors seem to be able to listen with such care that they are able to respond to each of the points raised in order, once the penitent has stopped speaking.

In some respects, the Mystery of Confession provides a unique possibility for communication, and the onus for this to take place lies firmly on the shoulders of the priest. He has to listen and to be present. He cannot walk away, answer the phone, or allow himself to be distracted in any other way.

Except in very exceptional circumstances, which will be described to you should they ever occur, the priest is not allowed to act on any of the information you tell him in confession. If there is some reason he wants to talk about something you mentioned in confession at a later date, he is supposed to ask your permission first, and if you say "no," that is the end of the matter.

There is an old story I have heard in different forms in different languages. A priest is tested by God when someone goes to confession and says that he has had copies made of the keys to a particular house. Later the priest discovers that it is, in fact, his own house that is being described. The end of the story varies, but it is basically aimed at demonstrating that a good priest would not then go home and have the locks changed. He behaves as if the communication during confession never existed.

The reality for most priests is that what people say in confession is forgotten as soon as the person leaves. It is one way the priest guards against living with too much pain and distress. If he does his job well, he will listen carefully to what is being said—listen with every fiber of his being—but then forget it all as soon as he reads or recites the prayers of absolution.

The priest is the witness of the penitent's confession. It is God who actually hears the confession; the priest does not stand in the place of God, and he certainly does not stand in judgment on the penitent. Such ideas do exist in other parts of the Christian world, but they are alien to Orthodox thinking and practice. Further, forgiveness in the Orthodox Church has nothing to do with paying for past transgressions. On the contrary, forgiveness is a free gift from God that can never be earned or merited—it can only be received. We do not confess to appease an angry God. We confess to make our relationship with a loving God real.

When the penitent approaches the icon or the confession desk (depending on the tradition), it is important to remember that there are actually two sinners standing there: one the penitent, one the priest. Since the priest is regularly at the center of a parish's relationship with God, his own sinfulness is perhaps all the more apparent to himself. Of those to whom much has been given, much will be expected, and the priest should have a very clear awareness of how far short of the required standards he himself comes. Sin is not alien to the person of the priest. Sin is alien only to God.

Ultimately, the importance of the Mystery of Confession lies in the difference it makes in the life of the penitent. Most sins have deep roots in a person's attitudes. Attempting to change attitudes is an all-but-impossible, monumental task, requiring the grace of God for its success. By entering the tent of mystery with the minister of the Church, the penitent has the opportunity to emerge changed, forgiven, sanctified, and restored to spiritual health. He or she often needs to leave the place of confession with some help and suggestions about how to change the way the present sins occurred. Forgiveness is wonderful, but it is not the end of the Mystery. The end of this Mystery is nothing less than transfiguration. The Mystery of Confession starts with estrangement and alienation from God, and ends with the path toward theosis.

The sort of advice that may have been given in the past may need to be reviewed in the light of what we now understand about the way the human personality works. Saying, "Don't do that; it's bad," is unlikely to change anyone's lifestyle, particularly if the person is struggling precisely with the matter being condemned.

Any statement that conveys the message, "If you do such and such a thing, you are a bad person," is also unlikely to produce change. The person will leave confession with a sense of doom and failure, whereas the goal is for the penitent to leave feeling that a change has already been accomplished, and his or her task is then to act on that change. Certainly, the priest has the opportunity to talk about the specific experience of the Orthodox Church on a given subject. But more often, he will want to give the penitent pointers, preferably from his own experience, as to how to effect a change, the desire for which has brought the penitent to the Holy Mystery in the first place.

❧ THE CONTENT OF CONFESSION ❧

Naturally, not everyone will use confession well, and there is no training for it, as such. If it is used in the service of the ego, the penitent might be tempted to try to impress the priest with his goodness (or badness!), and to use the time to justify any amount of antisocial or amoral behavior. This is not what the Mystery is for. Some people use the time to complain about their relatives, their station in life, and their problems. When this occurs, the priest can point out, gently but firmly, that the purpose of confession is to talk about sins, not about problems. The priest must take care to point out what is sin and what is not.

In general terms, spontaneous thoughts are not sins, spontaneous feelings are not sins, and temptations are not sins. Sin usually involves doing or saying something. Feeling angry is not a sin. Acting on feelings of anger may be a sin. A sudden impulse to steal is not a sin. Acting on that impulse almost certainly is.

Sometimes people will confess all sorts of things about other people, sometimes at great length, about what they have done wrong, what they said and did, how terrible they are, and so on. Then at the end, they say something like, "I felt angry about all these people," which is the "confession" part. One cannot repent of other people's sins.

The purpose of confession is to tell God (through the priest) of the sins we have committed. Naturally, God does not need us to tell Him our sins; He knows very well what they are before we open our mouths. However, there is something important and powerful about standing in front of another human being and doing the last thing in the world we want to do.

The human personality is a complex mechanism. It does not come naturally to us to talk badly about ourselves or to show ourselves in a bad light. On the contrary, in most situations we prefer to show ourselves in a good light—perhaps even better than we are in real life. We might exaggerate, or at least stress certain parts of our stories, in order to make ourselves look good. Our ego-strength generally lies in our ability to convince people that we are more or less perfect, if not that we are the most significant person on the planet. To do otherwise looks dangerous and unwholesome, and yet that is precisely what we are called to do in this Mystery.

However, there is another process going on at the same time. Even while we are building up a beautiful picture of ourselves and our achievements on the outside, there is often a dialogue continuing on the inside that is dragging us down as far, if not further, than our outer conversation is building us up. In reality, we often do not like ourselves nearly as much as other people like us. We often cannot see the good qualities other people can see in us, and we insist on believing that we are, in many respects, hopeless.

Of course, the tension between the outside speech and the inner dialogue causes us to be moody and neurotic. So many of us feel as if we are living a lie. "If you knew me as I really am, you would not like me" is one half of the story, and "You cannot live without me" is the other.

One of the aims of confession is to bring these two extreme statements closer together. We can show ourselves to God and to the priest as we really are, and the world does not come to an end. The priest does not run away shrieking and waving his hands in the air, but responds with love and encouragement.

At the time of confession, we are encouraged to be realistic and not to overstate the case against ourselves. We may be tempted to go to confession and paint the blackest possible picture, thinking that is what will impress the priest, or at least make it seem worthwhile to go to confession in the first place. The list of things people commonly raise in confession is quite a short one, and it is unlikely that many people would be able to go to a priest who has any experience and tell him something he has not heard many times before.

Honesty, not graphic detail, is what is required. It is not good to mention anyone else by name, for example. Other people are not in confession: you are. Of course, a child's reference to a parent or a best friend is fine, but naming names is not a part of the Mystery.

~: SIN AND RESPONSIBILITY :~

The concepts of sin and responsibility are intertwined at a very important level. In most cases, it is only possible to talk about committing a sin in situations where we have the choice whether to do so or not. In many cases, if there is no choice involved, there can be no sin either. In the language of the Church, we talk often about voluntary sin and involuntary sin, but the latter refers to sin of which we are unconscious at the time, when we operate on reflex or out of habit.

The burden of responsibility each of us carries is both extremely small and extremely large. It is extremely small, since it consists almost entirely of one's own person, one's own actions, and one's own aspirations. We spend a great deal of emotional and spiritual energy pretending that we are able to change the lives of others. This is a dream we sometimes pursue to the gates of hell. In fact, it is always difficult and usually impossible to change anyone else at all.

Some people even fall into the trap of maintaining that they could only find their own happiness or fulfillment in life if one or more of the people in their lives would change. This is rather like making a budget for the year ahead that is contingent on winning the jackpot in the lottery. People do not usually realize they are doing it, or how stupid it is to try to do it, until it is pointed out to them, and even then they often retreat behind a wall of denial.

The notion that "I can be happy/content/fulfilled/motivated/ successful only if everyone else in the world changes" lies at the heart of most people's sense of sadness and failure. It is completely illogical and impractical to try to make other people change, particularly in the way we normally attempt to do it—by telling them to change. That simply doesn't work.

There are some general exceptions to this observation, but they are not many in number. Parents of young children are in a special relationship, but even they by no means have complete control over whether or not the children emerge from infancy as good adults. Educators too, particularly of young children, have to examine their sense of responsibility carefully. Certainly, there is a chance that people will change if the path to change is attractive and made to look like something that will be of use. If, on the other hand, someone is confronted with the demand to behave in such-and-such a way for motives far from his or her own immediate advantage, the chances are that the demand will be ignored.

Incidentally, there are important reasons we should encourage children, even quite young children, to confess. The wisdom of the world will inform them soon enough that confession goes against nature. Children early on realize that "owning up" is not a sensible thing to do, and that when one does, the penalties are severe. Encouraging children towards honesty in early life, particularly within the Mystery of Confession, bears a great deal of fruit later on, when the stakes are higher.

So on the one hand, the area of responsibility carried by each individual is quite small. But on the other hand, it is huge: it encompasses almost everything within the circle that might be drawn around one's feet. Although this is where responsibility actually lies, most of us are anxious not to allow any sense of responsibility to come within this circle—the very place where it has some real force.

Often we would prefer to have no sense of responsibility over ourselves. This is where we invoke all sorts of other circumstances, people, situations, and notions to take the edge off the real responsibility that lies here. Here we try to shrug off responsibility, preferring to be responsible in other people's space, but declining to be responsible in our own. This is a dance of dazzling proportions. It leads to an inauthentic lifestyle and the further misery of the human race.

Obviously, then, the practice of confession with some frequency allows us to come to terms with our own responsibility and to see it in its rightful context.

The desire to ascribe some sort of magical quality to God's forgiveness must be avoided. If we think in logical and legalistic terms, someone who has just received forgiveness in confession and is then run over by a bus (or suffers some other immediate involuntary demise) is, by definition, a saint, whereas the person who goes home, has an argument with his wife, and then gets killed is, logically, a sinner for eternity.

The logic of this cannot be faulted, but it is not relevant to the issue. The forgiveness a person receives in the Mystery of Confession is a part—and only a part—of that person's complete relationship with God. Sanctity is not a state that depends on time, since time is "of this world." The same can be said of forgiveness, even if the exact meaning of this word is difficult to determine using the human mind. The logismoi flowing through our minds make little or nothing of forgiveness beyond the expectation that there must be some sort of catch. It is only the heart that can fully accept the forgiveness of God for what it is.

The Mystery of Confession is an important step on the path of transformation, towards the transfiguration that prefigures the essence of the life each person is invited to experience in Christ.

❦ CONFESSION AS RECONCILIATION ❧

The moment we are enrolled among the members of the Body of Christ, there is a sense of "less-than-perfect" about us. Is it ever possible to live up to our vocation? Is anyone a perfect Christian? Living in the state of spiritual disharmony that is the environment of fallen creation, our lives do not easily take on the characteristic of sanctity that closeness to the Person of Christ might suggest. The thoughts generated in our minds are hardly different from those of people who have no conscious contact with God, and sometimes if they are different, it is because they are worse. The thoughts that flow freely in our minds often seem far removed from wholesomeness, sanctity, and a deep sense of our security in God. Our hearts may respond to God's love, but most of us are stuck in our minds, and which of us is in tune with the voice of silence in our hearts on a day-to-day basis?

The standards of the early Church were often very high, and temporary excommunication from the life of the Church was imposed on those who, for whatever reason, were not acting as the Church thought they should. Originally, this was probably true of those who had committed grave sins and whose crimes were a matter of public concern. We can see from at least some of the writing in the New Testament that members of the Church were expected to live sinless lives after baptism. Indeed, in places St. Paul and other writers seem quite surprised that people should fall into sin after being incorporated into the Body of Christ. This is an indication, at the very least, of the expectation of the transforming power received when someone joined the Church, but in the course of time standards dropped, and the high moral tone proved to be somewhat impractical.

Once the Church became the "preferred religion" of the Roman Empire, and certainly in later circumstances where her faith was adopted as the religion of a state, it was almost inevitable that the fervent and expressive nature of faith was likely to subside. From being a close-knit, life-and-death, charismatic community, the Church sometimes fell victim to a mentality that stressed bureaucracy and organizational matters more than spiritual ones. In due course, the Church changed the way she felt about herself, even though the invitation to repentance never disappeared altogether, but rather went through a transformation, adjusting to the needs of the age.

The eternal mission of the Church is to return time and again to the words and example of Christ, the source of her life, and to rediscover what it means to live the life of the Spirit within the contemporary world. What is true for the Church as a whole is also true for each member individually, and the Holy Mystery of Confession gradually came to provide the precise solution for that precise need.

The very sanctity of Christ throws light on those factors that make us less-than-perfect in every level and dimension of our being. It is

here, in the fallenness of who we are, that the Mystery of Forgiveness is operative and available to each and every baptized person.
Not really to do with guilt or punishment, and not even essentially
to do with forgiveness, this Mystery centers on the process of being
brought back to the status we are given in baptism as children of the
living God. The central focus of this Mystery is exile and return, self-
imposed alienation followed by the opportunity for reconciliation.

Almost every human being is dissatisfied with her or his life. The
source of this dissatisfaction may be different on different occasions,
but it is rare for people to be able to be completely content with themselves just the way they are. Constantly in tune with the logismoi—
the stream of thoughts in our minds—most of us are subjected to a
constant barrage of pessimism that we have learned to accept as part
of life. Much more than simply choosing to see the metaphorical glass
as half-empty, we often assume that life is biased against us.

If to this sense of basic dissatisfaction and fear we add a list of
events and actions about which we are ashamed in our own lives, then
we have a pretty bleak picture of what it means to start out on the
path towards this Mystery.

The end of the journey, however, is far brighter. By going to confession, we receive forgiveness for sins we have committed in the
past, but we are left with the experience we have acquired. That is
to say, we leave behind all bad and negative feelings and thoughts
about things we have done, or things we should have done and did
not; but we retain the experience so that we can learn from it in the
future.

The story about the repentance of the prodigal son in the Gospel
is an obvious icon of what confession should be like. One surprising
aspect of this story is that the brother who goes off, sins, and then
returns is, in some important way, spiritually superior to the brother
who stays at home and lives an outwardly good, if unadventurous,
existence. The one who loses and regains life does so at a higher
level than the one who does not. That experience—of being lost and
found—then lives on and colors the whole of that person's life from
that time onwards. This is what happens to us each time we take part
in the Mystery of Confession.

Quite a lot of the high points of our lives revolve around the first experience of something. It can be demonstrated that in some sense we are always trying to recapture the blissful feelings associated with the beginnings of things that are important to us. The romance of a human relationship tries to hold onto or recapture the heady, exalted feelings associated with falling in love. In another, less positive example, the alcoholic is forever trying to recapture the pleasure of his first drink. Of course, it is impossible, and so he takes a second drink, and a third and a fourth. However, a great deal of what we do at the highest level of our being revolves around the act of trying to recreate the past.

Confession does exactly that. It recreates the innocence we had when we were lifted out of the baptismal font (whether this is a real memory or simply a useful starting point). That eternity-in-time of pristine innocence is something to which the Orthodox Christian is invited to return time and time again.

The ability to start over is a great blessing. Imagine what it must be like to be involved in a traffic accident. Afterwards, one might go through a series of thoughts, all of which start "if only . . ." Receiving absolution and forgiveness of our sins actually allows us to do just that: we can revisit the situation we were in before we committed a sin. This gives us a tremendous amount of freedom to come to terms with the person we really are.

It is good to leave the place of confession with a sense that a line has been drawn, and that we no longer have to be the person we were before confession took place. Unlike the rebirth that takes place at baptism, which can only be experienced once, the rebirth of confession takes us back to the moment after baptism and is available to us as often as we require it.

~: PENANCE, CANONS, & PUNISHMENT :~

Finally, a little word about instructions that may look like punishments which we may receive from the priest when we take part in the holy Mystery of Confession. We borrow the Western word "penance" to describe this process, although (as with "sacrament" and "repentance") the Western word is somewhat shallow and misleading, providing a trap for the unwary. A penance, in the Western sense, is something that is supposed to pay back, to recompense somehow, for the evil we have done. This concept is completely lacking in Orthodox theology, where forgiveness is accepted as a completely free gift from a loving God, not the grudging acceptance of someone's desires because they perform some sort of deed. God cannot be bought by our inconvenience.

However, at times in the life of the Church, it was not uncommon to give people tasks to perform to show that they were truly sorry for whatever sin they had committed. Although there are books that contain lists of such tasks, they are rarely enforced today. This is a matter for individual confessors to worry about, and it is their responsibility to administer these matters once a bishop feels confident that they have received enough practical and theoretical training.

Exclusion from Holy Communion, rather uncommon in the life of the modern Church, is not a punishment *per se*, but rather should be viewed as an encouragement to the individual to take a clear look at his or her priorities in life, and to develop a deep sense of longing to be reunited with the rest of the worshipping Church, which makes up the Body of Christ. Lack of communion, or more precisely, "excommunion," should be a source of grievous discomfort, but its aim is to bring the person to a sense of longing to belong once more.

It is always worth remembering, when dealing with any writings about rules, regulations, and punishments, that the view of law in the East differs dramatically from that we know in the West. This is dangerous ground since there will always be exceptions to any rule, and a great deal of subtlety is involved, even for those with black-and-white thinking.

In general terms, rules and regulations are used in the East to describe an almost perfect view of what society would be like in a perfect world. Rules are there to be consulted when things go horribly wrong, and the influence of those rules is then used to bring Christian society back into line with the precepts of the Gospel.

In the West, by contrast, rules (even laws) are seen as the regular day-to-day way we run things and are appealed to at the smallest infraction. If we drive through a red stoplight, we know we have a good chance of getting a citation. It is immediate, it is the law, and it is the Western way of doing things.

For this reason, people should exercise extreme caution when they look at books of rules and regulations, no matter how Orthodox the book appears to be.[13] A very senior and holy bishop once made the comment in my hearing that no convert should open such a book until he or she has been in the Church for thirty years. Most people would do well to leave canon law to the people who are experts in the field. It takes many years of study, but also many years of living an Orthodox life, in order to become qualified.

Ask a priest or a bishop if there is a problem in your own life, but do not be quick to apply any rule to yourself or to anybody else without consulting someone who is deeply within the tradition of the Orthodox Church. It is a great pity that some people join the Church, the ark of salvation, only to place all their faith in the sin-lists of medieval rigorists some months later. If a person needs to look for regulations, let him look first to the Gospels, particularly the Sermon on the Mount section of St. Matthew's Gospel (chapters 5–7).

---

13 I am thinking in particular of *The Rudder*, compiled by St. Nikodemos of the Holy Mountain, the same saint who compiled the Greek version of the *Philokalia*. This book collects many of the canons and regulations of the Orthodox Church, and it is an indispensable resource for the canon lawyer. However, the footnotes, which form no part of the original text, should be read with care, since they were written by a nineteenth-century Greek theologian whose views are rarely representative of worldwide Orthodoxy.

~: CHAPTER 12 :~

The Mystery of the Anointing of the Sick

A LITTLE WHILE AGO, I SPENT SOME TIME WITH A MAN who was dying of cancer. Though he was in his mid-seventies, this was the first time he had ever been seriously ill. He didn't really know how to act as a sick person, since he had never had any practice. His wife (and towards the end of his life, the nurses from Hospice) looked after all his needs, although he found this rather trying since he was not very good at saying what his needs were.

He had a form of cancer that was very painful, and as the days passed and his condition worsened, the pain increased. For him, the price of consciousness was extreme pain, since the pain-killing drugs he was free to take merely brought oblivion. He usually chose consciousness.

He had always been a self-assured man, and by hard work and determination, he had achieved a great deal in his life. He was quite aware of the nature of his condition, and he hated it. "Death stinks," he said, "but I guess cancer was the only way it could get my attention."

This particular man had to get sick in order to die. In a sense, the sickness occurred to help him die.

We cannot understand Christian living until we come to terms with Christian dying. Sickness is a foretaste of that death and a state of enormous spiritual significance.

Life presents us with all sorts of problems, and many of them are not easy. We tend to brush away anything that looks difficult or challenging, and it is possible for a human being to spend an entire lifetime out of focus, seeking dreams and other forms of unreality as if it were possible, through some divine oversight, to beat the system. In the end, though, there will be one or more factors that force us to look at reality just as it is. Sickness is one of the ways in which we are strongly encouraged to come into focus and to look at a variety of serious and important subjects: the significance of life, what it means to be alone, what it means to be dependent on other people, fear and desire, hope and anxiety, loneliness, isolation, and ultimately, death.

Illness and pain are not generally regarded as positive elements in our lives, and no one of good will would wish illness or pain on himself or on someone else. However, sickness and distress do get our attention. Sickness, in particular, accentuates the fact that we do not control our own lives. If, when we get sick, we respond by trying to grab even more rigid control of our lives, we are bound to fail. Sickness and physical death can occur at any time and are always unwelcome. However, when they occur, wanting and not wanting, based on our normal thought patterns, cease to be central to our lives, and the power of the ego with all its boisterous energy suddenly fades. As that happens, we are potentially able to deepen our awareness of God, our dependence on Him, and our desire to seek His will. Sickness and imminent death both present many opportunities for spiritual growth. Under the right circumstances, as shown in the Gospels, they are both factors through which God may be glorified.

In sickness, we have to learn to depend on others, even though we would prefer to be independent. The fact that we learn to be dependent at all (something we usually shrug off as childlike, if not childish) helps us develop or relearn a sense of dependence on God. We have to learn to sit back and be taken care of, rather than attempting to be in control. We certainly have the right to participate in our own healing, and the medical view, common in the past, that the doctor knew what was best for the patient is no longer so dominant. Nevertheless, the sick person, from a place of powerlessness, still has to learn to trust and to allow himself or herself to receive the available healing, no matter what happens. Healing leads to a new life; death also leads to a new life. We are involved in a very great mystery.

The Gospels stress two themes of major importance with regard to the subject of sickness. The first is that Jesus was a great healer. Many of the Gospel stories focus on His ability to heal. In bringing healing, He brought relief, comfort, and strength. The "Giver of life" is the God of healing, and we learn a great deal about our relationship with God in this way.

On the other hand, when the Gospels address the theme of sickness, we do not find the sense of rejection we might expect. Jesus shows that sickness is part of a greater picture. He uses the occasion of the healing of a blind man to present a strong teaching: far from being a punishment for sin (either that of the person who is sick, or that of his parents), sickness exists so that God might be glorified. St. Paul takes up the same theme in another context, where he shows that it is in our weakness that God's glory is shown. Pain and discomfort in the present moment find their significance and meaning for us in the glory of eternity.

This doesn't mean that God is somehow delighted by our pain or by our signs of weakness, but rather that when we acknowledge our weakness, which is so much easier to do in sickness than in health, the dimension of our dependence on God and His love for us is all the more apparent.

Mary, sister of Martha, said to Jesus of His friend Lazarus, "He whom You love is sick" (John 11:3). In times of sickness, when we uniquely have the time to take notice, God is like a parent sitting through the night at the bedside of a sick child, caring and waiting, watching for possible signs of improvement, perhaps ministering all the more intently when the only progression is downward.

Sickness can be the path to eternal life. Indeed, some people are only capable of finding eternal life through the experience of physical death. The specter of spiritual death has been destroyed once and for all, since Jesus "destroyed death by death." However, the physical death we experience at the end of earthly life plays its own part in our salvation. To push that death away is to push away life itself. Death in this context is the seal of life, which in turn allows us to grow and become transformed in ways we, in this life, can only guess at.

In the Mystery of the Anointing of the Sick, there is a strong awareness on behalf of the Church that the sick person is in the hands of God, and that God will provide healing. However, the prayers do not attempt to limit God in the way in which He chooses to give that healing. Far from being a rite to force God into a course of action—to make this patient well—the Mystery is rather a solemn commitment by the sick person, surrounded by the Church, to place himself or herself completely and without reservation into the hands of God.

The arrangement of the anointing in the Orthodox Church looks rather extravagant, calling for the presence of seven priests. In practice, it is rarely possible to pray this service exactly in the way it is presented in the books. However, this arrangement is a good indication of the importance the Church accords to this particular Mystery of God's grace.

Health is the state of balanced perfection we receive from God, and it is something with which we are entrusted. We participate in the condition of our own health to a large degree. However, asking for healing, we surrender to God, since in sickness, perhaps more than at any other time, we come from a position of powerlessness.

The pain of sickness is a great mystery. In some senses, the function of pain is to keep us focused. Pain is one of the few aspects of life that grabs our attention and keeps it grabbed. Most other forms of experience that demand our attention—beautiful sights in nature, for example, or particular pieces of music or poetry—are not nearly as efficient as pain in keeping us focused.

In a teaching of Jesus that we rarely mention (Matthew 5:39), He says, in effect, "Do not resist evil." The rigorous state of acceptance He envisages here is something quite beyond the capacity of our own will and determination. From the point of view of the mind, such an instruction looks preposterous.

However, in surrendering completely to God, such an action makes perfect sense. A possible interpretation is this: Jesus does not intend that we should give in to the evil impulses inside of us, but that we should surrender to forces outside of ourselves without labeling them, without first deciding what is "good" and what is "evil." This we can do only by submitting to what looks like evil, since we naturally tend not to resist the good. "Love your enemies" actually means "have no enemies." "Do not resist evil" means "learn to resist nothing."

We have a natural tendency to try to avoid pain and sickness. We are usually made aware of sickness through a symptom, which is not actually the illness itself, but rather a sign that an illness is present. A toothache, for example, gets our attention, but the toothache is not the sickness. Rather, the pain signals that there is an infection present. At this point, our natural inclination is often to try to rid ourselves of the symptom (the toothache) without doing anything about the sickness itself.

When we go to a doctor, we generally present him or her with a symptom to cure. The doctor's work is to discover what is causing the symptom, and then to attempt to cure the underlying condition. The problem the patient presents is not usually what actually needs to be cured.

When we extend this picture to our spiritual condition, it is possible to talk of sin as being symptomatic of some other, deeper spiritual disease. The method we generally try to follow is straightforward, but not very effective. We observe our sins, and then try to make ourselves well by eliminating the sin. In most cases, the sin is simply a signal that there is an underlying malaise, which can be characterized as being out of touch with God. This is the big sickness, compared with which individual sins are of little importance.

It is interesting that in participating in the Holy Mystery of Anointing, we receive the anointing with the words, "for the healing of soul and body." We are very quick to be aware of bodily ills, like a toothache. We are much less likely to rush to heal our underlying spiritual condition.

The words we hear at Holy Communion are similar, but add another dimension both to our sickness and to the healing we are about to receive. We receive the "precious Body and Blood of our Lord and God and Savior Jesus Christ, for the remission of sins, and for life eternal." The forgiveness of sin (of which remission is a part) is, as it were, the cure for the presenting problem, while the more general condition of being out of touch with God is healed through that mysterious expression "life eternal," which stands as a sort of shorthand for participation in the life of God.

For much of our lives, we expect to be in fairly good health almost all the time. We do not necessarily care for our bodies particularly well, eating a lot more than we need and exercising rather less than we need. So long as we have it, good health is often ignored, to the point where we only think about health when things go wrong and we get sick or are in pain.

Good health, however, can actually be a part of our prayer lives. At the very least, good health encourages us to be grateful, particularly after a period of sickness. Many a deep relationship with God has started with the words, "thank you." Saying "thank you" immediately gives us a framework within which the relationship develops, and that is what we are seeking to achieve. If our prayer life is nothing but a list of gripes and anxieties, there is little room for development. (Not that gripes and anxieties have no place in prayer. If we seek a real relationship with God, it has to include the less-than-perfect, as well as the bits of our lives about which we feel positive.)

Sickness may or may not be a test of our trust in God, but it is always an opportunity for spiritual growth. A sick person is sanctified in ways those who are well are not. Certainly, a sick person may devote more time to prayer, and do so in ways which are not available to others, including that most important factor of prayer which consists in merely relaxing in the presence of God.

However, sickness is for our spiritual good as well. Some time before I was ordained, I happened to be in the hospital for a whole month. I was in the middle of my teaching internship, which made life a little difficult, and I was also quite far from home, university, and friends.

At that time there was an Orthodox priest visiting Oxford from the Soviet Union. This was quite an unusual occurrence in those days, since the cold war was still ablaze. However, the priest turned out to be a very good pastor, and the little community in Oxford benefited considerably from his ministry for a number of years.

This priest came to give me Holy Communion during the time I was in the hospital, many miles from Oxford where he lived. I was surprised by his visit and touched by the efforts he had made to be there. We went down to the chapel in the hospital so that we would have a quiet place.

As a rather recent convert, I was well versed in all the rules and regulations of the Church, and protested that since I was not fasting, I would not be able to receive Holy Communion. The priest was quick to point out that on this occasion I was sick and in the hospital, and fasting would not be appropriate. This was particularly true since I was to receive Holy Communion as it were on his schedule and not by my own desire.

The next surprise occurred when I assumed I would make a confession and receive forgiveness before Holy Communion. The priest pointed out that I was a sick person, and that sick people find it difficult to sin, in comparison with people who are well. He felt confession was unnecessary at that time.

The Russian priest anointed me with oil that had been blessed in the church some time before during an anointing service. He then gave me Holy Communion, and after a short conversation he left. On that occasion I did recover from the illness I had, went on to complete my internship, and some years later I was ordained.

However, I also have to be aware that one day, by God's grace, I will be anointed and I will not recover from whatever physical condition is causing me trouble. That anointing, too, will be for "healing of soul and body," not an effort doomed to failure.

~: CHAPTER 13 :~

The Mystery of Marriage

It is perhaps no accident that Holy Matrimony is the one rite of the Church that is actually called a "mystery" in the Holy Scriptures. The presence of Jesus at the wedding in Cana is, in the tradition of the Church, indication enough that marriage is something wonderful and something to be treasured, a "great mystery" (Ephesians 5:32).

We need always to bear in mind that a large number of the most important commentators on the Orthodox life have been monastic men and women. It is hardly surprising that when monastics are writing for other monks and nuns, they tend to praise the virtues of chastity and celibacy and to be on guard against any possible infringement of those virtues. Nevertheless, the experience of the Church as a whole has never suggested that the monastic state is somehow spiritually superior to that of married people, and the theology of the Mysteries guarantees that the path to sanctity is open to the married person and the single person alike.[14]

---

14 On a personal note, I have to admit that participation in the Mystery of Marriage is outside my own experience. Not only are my comments here personal (as they are in the rest of the book) but they are also those of an outsider.

Perhaps the most interesting fact about marriage is that, without the help of God, it cannot work. What couples are trying to achieve is impossible, unless the grace of God is allowed to help.

Certainly, if marriage was difficult in times past, it is all but impossible now. There are many reasons for this. The vision of what marriage is all about has changed considerably since the Church was born over two thousand years ago. Even when we assume that certain things have remained constant—that people fall in love, that they subconsciously seek to prolong the species by having children—other enormous changes have taken place, mainly because of economic and sociological factors that have little to do with the experience of the Church, and more to do with society in general.

The immediate ancestor of Christian marriage is Jewish marriage, and the focus of Jewish marriage is to do with contracts. Two entire families are bound to each other through the man and the woman getting married. It is important to specify exactly what the financial and social implications of the marriage union are. This forms both a spiritual and secular backdrop to the experience of the Orthodox Church.

Another important factor is that almost everything Christian theology has to say about marriage and the family assumes the context of the extended family. The so-called "nuclear" family so common today is a modern invention, dating more or less from the time of the Industrial Revolution of the eighteenth and nineteenth centuries.

The trend away from the extended family continues today in those countries (which appear to be many) in which people, particularly young people, are leaving villages and going to look for work in the towns and cities. The factors causing this drift seem to be entirely economic, since it is probably true that it is easier to earn a living in a town than in the countryside. I well remember, many years ago, showing Montana to someone from California, who commented that there was no money to be made in Montana—there were simply not enough people there. Many young Montanans appear to agree—with their feet, if not in their hearts.

However, there are other important factors in the urban migration, some of which are not so obvious. People are actually abandoning a situation in which everyone knows them in favor of a situation where it is possible to be completely anonymous.

I experienced the lack of anonymity on a basic level when I was sent to live in the Monastery of St. John on Patmos. Having been born in a large city, I was used to living in a situation where most of the people I passed on the street on a daily basis were total strangers. On Patmos, not only was I an outsider, but everyone on the island had known everyone else on the island since they were born. I could not do or say anything without everyone seemingly getting to know about it. When I made a purchase in the village store, the other monks seemed to know all about what I had bought before I got back to the monastery. They were not being particularly intrusive, no matter how I felt about it. They were simply living their vision of everyday life, which included knowing almost everything about the lives of those around them.

Escape from this kind of situation looks attractive at first, as does any indication of personal autonomy and freedom. You go to the city, and no one knows or particularly cares what you get up to. After a while, however, a person can begin to notice that in this situation there is also no silent support, no caring. In the village, the interference of relatives and other villagers might be irksome. When everyone knows everyone else's business, tensions are bound to exist. However, in the city, when a problem comes along, there are no concerned neighbors and there is no hidden network of caring; in the city, people are expected to sink or swim on their own. In a real crisis, state agencies and curious neighbors are of little use compared with the safety net provided by village life. And village life provides support in everyday matters as well. In a village, childcare is almost never an issue. In a city, it is a major problem, underlying many of the difficulties faced by couples, generally in the earlier years of marriage when other issues also appear difficult.

Anonymity allows people to be more courageous in the ways they differ from their fellow citizens, and it may be partly for that reason that so many changes are occurring in people's lifestyles in the modern world. Change may or may not be good, but it always carries anxiety in its wake.

The answer to some of the problems posed by this sense of disintegration consists not in forcing people into lives of misery based on the model of the nuclear family, but in reviewing the importance of the extended family, and in adapting that as a model for community life in the future. It is likely that any new form of extended family will be different from the old, traditional one, since the older pattern is largely based on rural life, and the majority of human beings are no longer able to choose the rural environment.

The nuclear family is, unfortunately, a very difficult standard to live by. In an extended family, the various tensions that arise in normal family life tend to be diffused among its members. Sons and daughters are parented as much by grandparents, uncles, and aunts as by their own parents, who may be out working most of the time. In particular, the various problems Freud predicts as normative—boys with their fathers, daughters with their mothers—are made of less importance in the extended family, where it is possible for a boy to escape a source of constant conflict (perhaps with a father) and seek out the less "dangerous" company and counsel of a grandfather, an uncle, or even a cousin.

Tensions between the married couple are also magnified and exaggerated by placing that couple in isolation in a little box together with their children and all that they own. There is no escape, little room to retreat, and no place to hide. It is ironic, but largely true, that the nuclear family is designed to explode.

Place on top of this almost impossible situation a number of highly unrealistic expectations, as fostered in modern customs and traditions, and the situation becomes a great deal worse.

The commonly held belief that people get married because they are "in love" with each other makes marriage more difficult, not less. The fairy-tale romance followed by the "perfect" wedding and honeymoon are often viewed as the "happily ever after" ending of children's tales. The reality is that courtship and wedding are simply a prelude—often a pleasant one—to the hard work to come. Infatuation, the state of being in love, is not designed to last forever. But often couples who stop being in love with each other assume that they made a mistake, and they should not have married in the first place.

Love, by anyone's standard, is not essentially a feeling, but a decision. Feelings are wonderful and meaningful and poetic and sometimes contribute to a peak experience in our lives. However, they are also vapid, transitory, and often untrustworthy in conveying reality. The eye of the lover smitten with the beloved is not an eye that sees straight.

Genuine love that can sustain a lifelong relationship actually starts where infatuation leaves off. At that point, the fantasy of seeking for idealized happiness has disappeared, and it is slowly replaced by a more realistic expectation in which the process of love itself is manifested.

Another difficulty confronted by couples getting married is simply that marriage is now much easier to dissolve than was the case in earlier times. The statistics are not particularly helpful when a couple comes to a point where nothing less than hard work will keep the marriage going. When effort is called for, it is not helpful to see other marriages falling apart left and right.

Two people planning to get married have to examine their expectations carefully. Each will come to the marriage with an image of what marriage should be like—often based either on their view of their parents' marriage, or the very opposite of their parents' marriage. People assume that their partners have exactly the same view of marriage as they themselves do, even when they know that this is extremely unlikely. The final, sometimes fatal, expectation is that once married, people will have the right and the ability to change their partner to suit their own needs. In reality, this never happens.

This picture I am painting is purposefully bleak, because I feel it is better to go into marriage knowing that it is going to be difficult. In fact, marriage as we know it is impossible without God's help. The Mystery here is not an optional extra, but the very stuff of which a good marriage is made.

At this point, a brief history of marriage in the Church might be helpful. For a long period, marriage was regarded as a civil act, not one of particular spiritual significance. What was of significance was that the newly married Christian couple came to the church and there together took part in the Mystery of Holy Communion, both partners receiving the Body and Blood of the Lord. That action sealed the civil marriage in terms of the Church. The couple brought their decision to church, and it was blessed by taking part in the supreme experience of Christian living.

Sometimes we assume that a big decision, such as getting married, is somehow different from a small decision, such as choosing which shoes to wear. Unfortunately, that does not appear to be the case. No matter how complex a matter might be, and no matter how far-reaching its consequences, a decision is a decision. As human beings possess finite wisdom, no human decision is likely to be entirely correct or entirely wrong. Indeed, to be perfectly sure that one has made a good decision in any event is not a good sign.

A decision almost always carries with it a sense of regret, and the decision to get married is just as likely to carry this sense as is the decision to buy a particular refrigerator or automobile. If people are looking inside themselves for the "perfect" decision in getting married, they are setting themselves up for a ludicrously high set of expectations. These are likely to be dashed at the first sign of difficulty, causing the marriage to be abandoned when it has hardly begun.

A marriage relationship is, and remains, a matter of choice on a daily basis. A once-and-for-all attitude, commonly held in a Western setting where marriage is based on vows, is foreign to Orthodox life. In the Orthodox setting, a marriage is created each day, not fashioned at the wedding ceremony. The wedding ceremony is the Church's blessing on the work that starts there and then, not a standard of rigid determination pronounced on a work completed.

❦ THE MARRIAGE SERVICE ❧

The Orthodox wedding ceremony generally consists of two separate services joined together. Betrothal (engagement) is one thing and marriage (wedding) is another. Why it should be so is lost in the mists of time, but most cultures seem to have this two-stage process of getting married. Since marriage is older than Christian tradition, and indeed the Church seems to have been little concerned with it until comparatively late in her history, both betrothal and marriage have been incorporated into the blessings the Orthodox Church liberally dispenses in the name of God to those who seek them.

In modern usage, the two services are celebrated together, with an engagement blessing of a fairly informal nature taking place weeks or months earlier outside the church building, and then being repeated officially at the start of the marriage service. It appears some confusion existed in the minds of some laypeople as to when the marriage became official, and since this matter has serious legal and social implications, the Church decided to solve the problem by putting the two services together. Now everyone knows that the couple is not actually married until they have taken part in both ceremonies.

The first service, the betrothal, has as its central theme the blessing and exchanging of rings. Rings have all sorts of symbolism, but the one the Church concentrates on is the role rings have played in various biblical stories. This sets the tone of both the betrothal and the marriage, since both are packed with references to events in both the Old and New Testaments. In order to appreciate the full depth of what is being said, it might be good for the bridal couple (and anyone else involved) to spend some time reading the various episodes in the Bible referred to in the service. When listened to with inner stillness, such reading is most beneficial to spiritual development.

Once the rings are in place, the service quickly moves on to the marriage itself. The prayers for peace are recited for a second time (with small differences), then two long, beautiful prayers, the second of which is particularly full of references to marriage in Holy Scripture.

The joining of hands, followed by the crowning, lies at the heart of the service. In a mystical way, the two people become one flesh (though, of course, not one person!), and having done so through the joining of hands, they are "crowned" to each other. To most people living in the West, this does not mean much until it is witnessed.

The crowns, like the rings, are full of symbolism. Here the Church becomes a little more subtle and suggests two major themes: glory and honor (such as one might expect at a coronation), but also martyrdom. A martyr is called to witness to Christ with every ounce of his being, and both the bride and groom will need to learn to emulate that behavior if the marriage is to be successful. The themes of honor, restraint, social responsibility, and harmony flutter through the words of the service, giving active lessons as to how to bring the marriage to fruition.

These lessons include the epistle reading, in which St. Paul calls marriage a "great mystery." In describing what a marriage looks like, he uses the image of the relationship between Christ and His Church. Here we need to bear in mind what St. Paul was referring to as the Church. For him the Church was no institution, had no buildings, no social influence (except on her own members), and not much interest in the political and social life of the times. Rather, he saw the Church as a select group of people waiting impatiently for the second coming of the Lord, which was expected at any minute. People who are expecting the end of the world to occur very soon do not place a great deal of significance in marriage. Marriage is a long-term, generational matter, and would be pretty much irrelevant if today were to be the last day of your life. Having come to this awareness, we are ready to hear him say, "It is better to marry than to burn" (1 Corinthians 7:9)!

The epistle we hear in the marriage service (Ephesians 5:22–33), with its seeming bias towards male leadership in the marriage, is balanced somewhat in a Greek practice (not encouraged or sanctioned by the Church) in which the bride attempts to stamp on the toe of the groom at this point. She thereby takes her "power" in the face of the physically stronger male, and becomes, at the very least, an equal member of the partnership.

The Gospel reading in the service (John 2:1–11) recounts the central, most important event in the Church's understanding of marriage, which occurred when Jesus Himself attended a marriage at Cana in Galilee. He had been invited, together with His disciples. His mother was also there.

This provides us with one of the rare glimpses we have of anything approaching domesticity in Jesus' life. The Gospels are keen to give us a picture of His mission, His message, and the key events of His life, but we are left wondering what life was like in the small details—the level at which we recognize our own existence. Here in Cana, not far from the village of Capernaum, the place He called home, we can see that there was indeed some human interaction in His life, and that He did not live in a social vacuum.

There is an obvious social context here, since Jesus and His mother were invited. His brothers and sisters are not mentioned, nor His father, Joseph, and the Gospel writer does nothing to pander to our curiosity. However, since Jesus was invited with His disciples, there is obviously a spiritual context also. Whoever invited Jesus did so not just as a family friend, but in the context of Jesus' mission.

Equally lacking from the story in St. John's Gospel is any commentary that might show something of Jesus' views on marriage. There is a puzzle here, since Jewish tradition sees marriage as the norm if not a necessity, ordained by God and the subject of the very first commandment in the Torah. Yet, Jesus is not married, and no comment is made on that subject here or elsewhere in the Gospels.

Our inquisitiveness should not blur the tremendous significance of what happened at Cana. Here, in verbal iconic form, we are presented with a powerful teaching about the power of marriage to transform the individual. People may or may not be good, may or may not be wise, but alone they are like ordinary water. In marriage, they can, through the intervention of God, be transformed into "good wine" in a process which can only take place at a miraculous, "mysterious" level.

If we listen carefully to the words of Jesus in the Gospels, we often find that they have a sense of mystery wrapped around them. His words often reflect situations in which God interacts with mankind, not just on an obvious and natural level, but also in a profound personal way. It is here, in the deepest parts of the person which only God is able to reach, that the word "mystery" most often has its context. The mind does not like mystery. The heart knows that mystery is the fullest expression of our relationship with God. It is as it is, because God chooses to do it that way.

After the completion of the Scripture readings, the Lord's Prayer follows, surrounded by other prayers, as is the custom in the Orthodox Church. The words of Christ, which are the Lord's Prayer, are accompanied and surrounded by other prayers, acting like angelic support for the sacred words.

A cup of wine is blessed and then given to the newly married couple. The wine, representing the whole panoply of food, nourishment, joy, sharing, and encouragement, is drunk. Some have suggested that this is a remnant from the times when the couple came to church for Holy Communion and cemented their marriage in that fashion. However, I cannot imagine any circumstance in which the Church would replace the life-giving Blood of Christ from the holy chalice of Holy Communion with another, simple cup of blessed wine. More likely, I think, is a connection with the drinking of wine in the Jewish marriage service.

The procession around the table that follows, reminiscent of the procession around the font at Holy Baptism, allows the couple to take their first steps together blessed by God, guided by the Church, and supported by all the people who have come to be present and give the couple their prayerful encouragement.

After the crowns are removed, more blessings are recited, and then the bride and groom meet the world as a married couple for the first time. Filled with blessings, they leave the church. And the real work of being married begins.

~: A PAUSE FOR CONSIDERATION :~

The mood of a wedding service in church is often far removed from its spiritual significance. Sometimes it seems that the most important person at the ceremony is the photographer, that the rules of etiquette are more important than the words of the service, and that somehow the idea that it is the "bride's day" turns the occasion into a sad display of ego-expansion.

It is such a pity when a Mystery becomes nothing more than a mere ceremony. A ceremony is something people come to watch, whereas a Mystery is, both in principle and in practice, something in which people take part. Admittedly, some roles are more obvious than others—the priest has a specific role to play, and the bride and groom are obviously the focus of attention. However, everyone present is invited to take part and not simply to watch. Even if the task is merely to pray for the couple, that in itself is of great importance.

The flowers, the dresses, the bridesmaids, and the photographs should pale in comparison with the real task at hand, which is to present a decision—a human and fallible decision—into the hands of God and ask Him to create the miracle of married life.

If the Mystery is not the focus of the activity, the vainglory of the world is quick to fill the vacuum. When entire families get together—and in a marriage it is often a matter of two entire families getting together—there are often tensions, and people may concentrate on those. Any of a million distractions might make the day memorable, though far from spiritual.

Three occasions stand out in my memory. In the first, the mother of the bride arrived for the wedding rehearsal fifty minutes late, carrying aloft one of those rather tedious middle-class books of wedding etiquette, exclaiming that she wanted the wedding to be just "like this." It wasn't.

On another occasion, I was telephoned by another bride's mother, a woman I had never met. It was quite obvious that she regarded the church as a sort of wedding shop at which she simply ordered the things she wanted and skipped things that did not look attractive. She didn't want crowns at her daughter's wedding, though I cannot now remember why. We had crowns.

On a third occasion, a marriage consultant had been hired to look after the wedding. When we met in the church, she told me that she was going to put in a rose bower right over where the couple would stand, and that she wanted piped music from various show tunes to "set the mood." She got neither wish.

One of the great blessings in the Orthodox Church is that we do not have to create occasions. The Orthodox wedding service is so powerful, so profound, that we do not have to dress it up, give it atmosphere, or otherwise make it other than it already is. This allows people to relax. They may have problems at the wedding reception—crowds and alcohol are always a bit risky, and banquet food is rarely worth the money—but the marriage service of the Orthodox Church is a glimpse of heaven without making any particular fuss or effort at all.

~: CHAPTER 14 :~

The Mystery of Ordination

Two features of the Mystery of Ordination made a strong impression on me the very first time I was present at an ordination service in an Orthodox church.

The first is that ordination always takes place within the Divine Liturgy. Here, one Mystery is wrapped entirely within another. Among the sacred rites of the Church, this is a unique feature. No other Mystery—not even chrismation, which is usually celebrated together with baptism, but not always—is dependent on another in the same way. However, coming to terms with the link between ordination and the Divine Liturgy is of paramount importance in appreciating the role and function of the priestly ministry within the Church.

It is in the Divine Liturgy, as well as in other Mysteries and prayer services of the Orthodox Church, that the clergy—bishops, priests, and deacons—find their distinctive role. In the other major form of the Church's prayer, that of the locked room of which Jesus speaks (Matthew 6:6), the role of priesthood plays little or no part; in their private prayer lives, there is no distinction between priest and layman, and the clergy are on the same spiritual level as everyone else. Some of the major teachers of Orthodox spirituality, right up to our own times, have been lay people.

In the public worship of the Church, however, the clergy have a distinctive and essential role to play. This function carries over somewhat into the nonliturgical life of the Church, so that in some times and places the clergy have become administrators and (for various political reasons) social leaders too. However, this is not their central role. It is in the liturgy that their ministry has an essential quality; it is in the liturgy that priesthood has both form and function.

~: THE CANDIDATE FOR ORDINATION :~

The second feature in the service that caught my eye, easily missed if one is not looking for it, is that just before the ordination takes place, the candidate is grabbed by the arms by two men belonging to the order to which he is about to be ordained, and in this state he is presented to the bishop. Although "grabbed" might seem extreme, this gesture signifies that the candidate for ordination is presumed to be opposed to what is going to happen, and thus needs to be captured and coerced so that the ordination can take place.

Obvious among the many possible reasons for being opposed might be that the man feels unworthy of the grace about to be given to him. And he is right. No one is worthy of the grace of ordination, before or after it has taken place. The priestly ministry, at all levels, always sits on top of a human being, and the perfection of the former is always in tension with the fallibility of the latter.

In certain times in the Church's history, not all of them in the distant past, reluctance to be ordained signified more than anxiety about personal unworthiness. Ordination carried with it a promise of almost certain martyrdom, or at least persecution.

The Church thus assumes that a person is ordained in spite of his own desires. Only in this way is there a real possibility of a transformation through the grace of God, which would not be possible in a man who was bound (by his own ego) and determined to seek the priesthood for his own ends.

Of course, it is entirely possible to become a priest (or deacon, or bishop) for all the wrong reasons, and with motives far removed from sanctity. Some men may feel a need to be seen as a leader. To others, the dignity of the priesthood looks attractive. Indeed, there could be any number of wrong reasons, but even to understand that, the

The notion of vocation, such a feature in writings about ministry in the West, is not one of prominence in the practical life of the Orthodox Church. There is no talk in Orthodoxy about discerning a call from God. Orthodox tradition has little to say about an individual call from God to do anything. That would imply a certainty on the part of the individual as to what the will of God is, and Orthodoxy recognizes no such certainty.

Individuals, from patriarchs down, have no sense of personal indisputable rightness in the Orthodox Church. That is why the doctrine of papal infallibility is so abhorrent to Orthodox sensibilities. Certainty belongs only to the Church as a whole, but even then, it is experienced gently and tentatively. Ecumenical Councils, the highest authority in the Church during the period from the earthly life of Jesus until the Second Coming, are able to make proclamations about all sorts of things, but even they reach the status of infallibility only after their decisions and decrees have become an integrated part of the life and experience of the Church. This baffling, paradoxical way of working through problems is an integral part of Orthodox life.

Far from being the response to an inner call on the part of the ordinand, ordination happens, essentially, at the request of the Church, based on the needs of the Church at any given time. It does not depend fundamentally on the mental or even spiritual disposition of the candidate, but on the need of the Church to have priests. In this respect, the ministerial priesthood of the Church lies in strong contrast to the monastic life, which has not only an entirely different function within the Church, but is also based on an entirely different frame of reference.

According to the commonly expressed opinions of the monks of Mount Athos, monasticism is the simple offering of the person to God to live a particular life according to particular rules and norms. There is little talk here either of vocation or of the person answering a call from God to the monastic life. On the contrary, monasticism is a freewill offering which anyone can make at almost any time. There are no age limits for young or old, except insofar as is deemed wise according to the norms of the time.

For priesthood in all its degrees, the matter is entirely different. The Holy Canons are quite explicit about the sort of person who is eligible for ordination, including how old they need to be.

The way this process is expressed in practice is very interesting. The candidate for ordination has to approach a "spiritual father." (Here the expression does not necessarily refer to a spiritual giant, but rather to a person who has been blessed to hear confessions.) In many cases, the confessor and the candidate will already have been in a spiritual relationship, perhaps for some time. The prospective candidate then makes his confession—an intimate and frank appraisal of his life. The spiritual father may make enquiries regarding certain areas of life in which the Holy Canons make specific and sometimes stringent demands of the candidate.

Naturally, this whole process is regulated by the honesty of the candidate and the wisdom of the spiritual father. Sometimes there may be serious questions about the candidate's eligibility for ordination, which may be quite separate from issues of suitability. There may be occasions when certain rules are relaxed, and others when the same rules are applied with rigor. This is not a juridical process— confession can never be that—but a pastoral one. Paramount is the need of the Church, not the need of the individual, for ordination.

Whatever takes place in this sacred encounter between the candidate for ordination and his chosen spiritual advisor is, like all such encounters, clothed in privacy. The spiritual father may require the candidate to disclose certain details of his life to the ordaining bishop, since it is the bishop who must, in the end, make the decision to ordain. The spiritual father may or may not apply the full force of the canonical rulings regarding the priesthood, but if he is to give an affirmative response, he has to sign a document (called, in Greek, *symmartyrion*), which is then presented to the ordaining bishop. This document is a statement from the father confessor that the candidate is fit to be ordained.

Thus, even before ordination, a double layer of support is in place for the young priest-to-be: that of the bishop who ordains him, with whom he will have a special, though not necessarily very close, relationship; and that of his spiritual father, which is preferably of a deep,

spiritually intimate nature. Thus, the public and the private face of
the Church are both represented, answering to the two separate
though related prayer lives of the Body of Christ. Public worship, and
most especially the Divine Liturgy, the prayer which leads to words
and actions, is represented by the bishop. The "prayer of the closet,"
the secret prayer of which Christ speaks, which leads to a profound
silence in the heart of the individual, is represented by the spiritual
father.

~: ON CLERICALISM :~

Clericalism, an impression that only the clergy are truly "in the
Church" and lay people are merely spectators, is not part of Ortho-
dox life. When it is sometimes encountered, it is almost always due to
Western influence, particularly from Roman Catholicism.

In Orthodoxy, the priesthood is not a tool of power, much less a
social or administrative class. Rather, it is the agent through which
the experience of God in the Holy Mysteries is made available to the
members of the Body of Christ. It is a dignity of service, not of supe-
riority. The youngest child present at a Divine Liturgy has a function,
one might even say a priestly function, just as much as the man in
vestments standing at the altar. The only difference is that the Church
has chosen that particular man to fulfill that particular function.

This situation is most clearly seen in village life in Orthodox countries. Here a priest is likely to be a farmer, like almost everyone else
in the village. According to the canons, he may not be a shopkeeper,
a banker, an innkeeper, or anything else that would involve competition, moneymaking, or special interest. Competition, even on a com-
mercial level, is deemed to be incompatible with the priestly life.

On Sundays and feast days, this man heads for the church instead
of for his fields, as he does the rest of the week. He may have no more
knowledge of theology than the other villagers, and may even have
to read the liturgical texts phonetically, without much understanding. Nevertheless, he is the priest, and he is usually given the benefit
of the doubt by the other members of the village. He does not hear
confessions, and he does not preach. These two tasks require special

training and a blessing from the bishop. However, the priest performs all the other necessary functions of the priesthood for his flock.

When such a man dies, the village might send his son off to the bishop for ordination, or they might choose one of their number they consider suitable for the task.

This pattern of Orthodox life is fast disappearing, as university credentials and other professional training are developed through most of the Orthodox world. It has to be remembered, though, that professionalism leads to clericalism, and clericalism is at odds with Orthodox experience.

As the many hundreds of years of history of the Orthodox Church testify, most Orthodox priests have been trained not in seminaries, but "on the job," directed by bishops and more experienced priests. Academic rigor or accomplishment may, in certain circumstances, be deemed desirable, but it is not a prerequisite to ordination in the Orthodox Church. Indeed, there is a danger that the priesthood may be looked upon as simply one profession among many, if the main emphasis is on qualifications and social standing. As with everything else to do with the Orthodox Church, the significance and importance of the priesthood is deeply grounded in mystery.

On occasion, bishops, who are the ministers of this Mystery and must correspondingly take responsibility for their sacred acts, choose to ordain people the world might find quite unsuitable. Such charismatic actions may indeed come to fruition, since the power of ordination is through the work of the Holy Spirit, and that power is without limit.

～ THE BASIS OF MINISTRY ～

In each of the degrees of the priesthood, the ordaining prayer is similar: "The Divine Grace, which always heals that which is infirm and completes that which is wanting, elevates, through the laying on of hands, the most devout deacon N. to be a priest. Therefore let us pray for him, that the grace of the All-holy Spirit may come upon him."

This prayer beautifully and succinctly sums up the Church's awareness about what is actually happening at an ordination. Human

achievement cannot attain the priesthood except by the grace of God.
What is lacking is made good; what is not required is overlooked.

Of course, this refers to the ordained man's actions as a priest, functioning within the Church, playing his defined role for the sake of the Kingdom. His own spiritual path and development are not affected in any way. The struggles taken into ordination are the struggles that remain after ordination. Priests who gossip, who are judgmental or power-hungry, arrogant or self-opinionated, greedy or immoral do not disturb the work of the Holy Spirit; they just make that work less obvious to the rest of the world. To identify the priesthood too closely with the ego, the mind-centered life-story, of the individual ordained is to stultify the work of the Holy Spirit. This is particularly true in the upper echelons of church organization, where there is a danger that the exercise of the ministry may be mistaken for the exercise of personal power—not only by outside observers, but by the clergyman himself.

The act of becoming a priest partly involves the obliteration of the self, in the sense of the words of the Forerunner, "He must increase, but I *must* decrease" (John 3:30). The priest is neither shaman nor oracle; he is not called to be a man of organization so much as a man of prayer. He should be approachable to those he serves, but always aware that he is at his best when allowing the grace of God to work through him unimpeded.

When he hears confessions, the priest should be deeply aware of his own sinful disposition, and when he blesses he is but a channel, allowing the grace of God to flow. When he says the prayers that change the bread and wine into the Body and Blood of the Lord, he should watch in amazement as God effects the transformation. Under older, less loving arrangements, such direct confrontation with God would have necessitated death. In the new covenant, the identity of the Body of Christ, both in the chalice and in the body of the Church, is made manifest and accomplished through the grace of God, who allows Himself to be influenced, perhaps even manipulated, by the prayer of the priest on behalf of the people.

The priest is also privileged to witness the transformation of the people he serves, which occurs simultaneously with the transformation of the bread and wine on the altar.

The priest should make every effort to be fully present when he is celebrating the Holy Mysteries. The mind loves to make excursions during times when the priest is so used to doing what he is doing that he distances himself quite unconsciously from his actions. The act of being present, which almost always has to start as a conscious effort, is fundamental and precious. The act of surrendering to God in this way is the gate to the Kingdom of heaven. In this mindless, ego-free presence, the priest becomes what he already is—a channel of God's grace. This process is available to any member of the Church at any time, but is most clearly seen in the liturgical priesthood. The degree to which a priest's own ego is engaged is precisely the degree to which the work of God's grace is hindered.

~: THE DEACON :~

The diaconate, as the first level of priesthood is called, presents many interesting features. Although a member of the clergy, when a deacon dies, he is buried as a lay person.[15] His is the only order of the priesthood that cannot bestow a blessing. However, in his task of presenting the offerings of the people, including the bread and wine, his role has very priestly overtones. At home in the altar as he is among the faithful in the body of the church, he is seen as an angel flying between heaven and earth.

Though not a source of authority in the same way that priests and especially bishops are, the deacon most clearly typifies the idea of priesthood as *diakonia* (service), from which his title derives. Although he must seek a blessing from a priest or bishop to perform his sacred mission and cannot perform services on his own, nevertheless, the dignity of his ministry is very sacred indeed.

Deacons are mentioned in the earliest writings about the Church, when they had (as they still have) a number of specific tasks, both in the liturgy and in the community. In the former they are the

---

15 This detail is obscured at the present time in the Greek-speaking Orthodox world, since one funeral service is used for all. In the past, there were special services for priests, bishops, and some others.

go-betweens, leading the people in prayer one moment, serving the needs of the bishop or priest inside the altar the next.

The form of prayer most often assigned to the deacon is the litany. The deacon stands at the front of the church, facing east, and invites the people to pray for a wide variety of situations and needs. In each case, the prayer itself is not the invitation ("For the peace of the whole world, for the good estate of the holy churches of God" and so forth), but the words "Lord, have mercy," which are sung by the choir and sometimes the people at the end of each petition.

From some older texts, we see that deacons also had the task of keeping order in churches. Now when they say to the people, "Let us attend," and "Again and again in peace let us pray to the Lord," they are providing necessary and important reminders for the people to concentrate their efforts, to be present in every sense of the word, and to participate in the work of the Church at that moment. At no point are the people treated as spectators. Just before the great offering of the bread and wine, the deacon admonishes the people, "Let us stand aright; let us stand in awe; let us attend, that we may make the holy offering in peace."

Unlike some other traditions, it is not customary in Orthodoxy for someone who is not a deacon to take the part of the deacon. The deacon has a distinct role and a distinct ordination. Only a deacon can take the part of the deacon.

However, should the deacon be ordained to a higher order, he nevertheless retains the status of the diaconate in addition to receiving the grace of the ministry of a priest or bishop, since all of the priestly work of the Church is based on his service. This is particularly true in regards to the second important role of the deacon, that of philanthropist. It is his task to care for the members of the community who need care, and to represent the Church as a whole in solving the ever-present problems with which society confronts it.

~: THE PRIEST :~

The use of the word "priest" is not as prevalent in the early life of the Church as it was to become later. In the New Testament, this word is almost always reserved for the priests of Judaism. The priesthood in Judaism is hereditary, and most of the functions of the priests were restricted to the temple in Jerusalem. After the fall of Jerusalem and the destruction of the temple some forty years after the Resurrection, the significance and power of the Jewish priesthood diminished. A newer class of religious professionals, the rabbis, who specialized in the study of the Law, became the leaders within Jewish communities.

The New Testament word for "priest" in the Christian sense is "presbyter," which has the connotation of "elder." As might be expected, the clearest picture of what elders do is found in the Divine Liturgy. In the collective subconscious of the Church, the bishop of each city celebrates the Sacred Mysteries on a regular basis at his cathedral, surrounded by his elders and assisted by the deacons, in the presence of the people of God.

Naturally, the needs of the Church changed as the years went by. It was only a matter of time before churches in the suburbs needed more attention, and so the elders were sent to outlying districts to serve a liturgy. However, when they did so, it was quite plain that the presbyter was merely a stand-in for the bishop, and although the liturgy at which he presided was complete, it was something like an echo of the liturgy celebrated by the bishop. As the Church grew, the bishop tended to become a more distant figure, seen by the people only on special occasions.

To this day, a priest serves the liturgy as a stand-in for the bishop. On the holy table of each Orthodox church there has to be an *antimension*, a special tablecloth signed by the bishop, which acts as a license by the local bishop for the Divine Liturgy to be celebrated in that place.

In the course of the liturgy, we pray many times for the hierarchy, but we also pray for the "brotherhood"—the entire body of the Church. The Church has these two dimensions at all times, even though the balance between the two is sometimes difficult to achieve.

The hierarchical dimension is expressed particularly in the Greek tradition, where in a local parish only the local bishop is named in the course of the prayers. At the bishop's liturgy, he commemorates his immediate superior—very often an archbishop—and in turn the archbishop commemorates his superior, usually the patriarch. In his turn, the patriarch, in what can become quite a lengthy process, commemorates all the other heads of Orthodox Churches throughout the world.

In this way, the catholicity of the smallest parish is ensured, since, through its bishop, it is connected to the Orthodox Church worldwide. This method also points to the completeness of the Church in even its smallest expressions. Belonging to a worldwide Church does not detract from the fact that a parish, in communion with a bishop, is complete.

One way in which hierarchy is expressed is in the simple matter of giving blessings. A blessing is a statement, sometimes an authoritative statement, that something is allowed, or that something has been set aside for particular use within the Body of Christ. Blessed water, for example, looks and tastes like regular water, but it has been blessed, that is, set aside by the Church, for a particular use in bringing the grace of God to people and objects it touches. Sometimes a blessing means no more than a "thank you," as in the blessings a bishop gives to the deacon when the latter censes him in the course of services. At other times, a blessing is tantamount to giving permission for something to happen, as when a priest blesses the robes of a deacon or an altar boy before they are put on.

However, there is an element of hierarchy here, too. A bishop blesses everyone, except another bishop, but a priest does not bless a bishop or another priest. Deacons do not bless anyone, although according to the canons, it seems that they have tried to do so in the past. In general, lay people do not give blessings, with the possible exception of a parent, who (in the tradition of Isaac in the Old Testament) might bless her or his child.

There is a sense, too, that the order of priesthood is more important than any particular person who holds it. During concelebrations, there may be any number of bishops, priests, and deacons present, yet only one member of each order actually performs the words and actions of the liturgy at any one time, the members of each order taking it in turns to do so according to somewhat complicated rules of seniority. The others simply stand, present.

Of all the orders, it is the vestments and ceremonial of the bishop that have been the most affected by changes in history. This sometimes makes it difficult to see the earliest mission of the Church being carried out in the modern world. There are two major areas of change, generally reflecting the role of bishop as archpastor. To see this clearly, we can turn to the architecture of some of the earliest churches. Architecture in general, and liturgical architecture in particular, often gives very strong clues as to the depth of the experience of the Church. One particular example is most apparent when looking at the throne of the bishop.

In some of the oldest extant Orthodox buildings, the place of the bishop was sitting on his throne behind the altar, surrounded by the *presbyteroi*, the elders, who sit beside him on each side, with the deacons standing at either end of this *synthronos*. This arrangement has a great deal to tell us about the way the Church thought about the place and ministry of the apostles shortly after the birth of the Church.

The collective memory of the Church, mentioned earlier, is still important. The tradition of the synthronos behind (to the east of) the altar table gives shape to much that we still do in our churches, even though the synthronos is rarely seen—either because it is now hidden by the icon screen, or because it has fallen out of use altogether. In any event, it was normal perhaps only in the chief churches of a city. It may never have been present in a good many smaller churches, where it would be unlikely that the bishop with all his clergy would ever congregate.

When the bishop sits on his throne surrounded by his presbyters, the icon of the hierarchy of the Church is complete. Here the bishop represents Christ sitting with His disciples, attended by the deacons of the community.

At some time, possibly around the Fall of Constantinople in 1453, a change—by Orthodox standards, a fairly drastic change—occurred when the chair of the bishop was moved out into the body of the church, to the place where the patriarchs had a throne, opposite that of the emperor in the Great Church. By this time, the icon screen had grown to a size that made the original importance of the synthronos difficult to appreciate. However, when the bishop sits on a throne outside the altar area, as happens in a number of our churches, the icon of the church hierarchy undergoes a subtle yet important change. Here the priests and deacons who attend the bishop are given a new role—one of political, not spiritual, origin. The presbyters and deacons now are courtiers standing guard in the presence of the bishop.

The second development was the adoption of imperial vestments, probably first by the patriarch (who took on an important role as ethnarch of the Christians in the new Turkish Empire), then by metropolitans, and then by all bishops everywhere. The two garments of particular concern are the *sakkos* (the tunic) and the crown-shaped miter, both of which were originally worn by the Byzantine emperor.

In the older tradition, clearly seen in icons, bishops wore the *omophorion*, the distinctive vestment of the bishop, over the *phelonion*, the normal vestment of the priest. The omophorion, whose shape suggests a lamb being carried upon the shoulders of a shepherd, distinctly brings the pastoral nature of the episcopal office to mind. This is a living out of the experience of the Church, which sees the bishop as the pastor within his diocese and the elders (the presbyters or priests) as his representatives in the churches of the diocese.

I would hazard a guess that if St. John Chrysostom were alive today, he might see the removal of the *ambo* (raised platform) in the middle of the church as a negative feature (although he often did not preach from there himself), but he would probably see the gradual development of the icon screen as something that had merit. However, he would likely be shocked to see all bishops dressed in the vesture of an emperor, complete with the imperial sakkos and an emperor's crown.

It is not by mistake that the Orthodox Church chooses its bishops from the monastic clergy. However, in the modern Church, it is relatively uncommon for bishops to come straight from a monastery. Instead, there has emerged (over many centuries) a two-tiered monastic system. One tier consists of monks who live their lives in a monastery with all the discipline and order that life entails. The other tier consists of a group of priests who are not married, who may or may not have taken monastic vows, and who form a cadre out of which future bishops are taken.

Such priests may be found working directly with bishops in administration, but some of them are also parish priests, living a life that approximates to that of the celibate clergy of other denominations. As such, they are an anomaly, the exact representatives of the class of priests the mind of the Church seems to want to avoid. The experience of the Church desires that all clergy should belong to a family, either a normal one (with a wife and children) or a monastic one. The priest with his family living amongst the families of the parishioners is a clear social statement, whereas the priest living alone is not. The lifestyle of a priest-bachelor is not something the rules of the Church take into account.

Monasticism has never been considered superior to the married way of life, yet by choosing bishops from among the monks, there has been a tendency to ensure that the monastic view of life is given plenty of support within the Church as a whole. Perhaps the days will return when bishops are chosen once more from among those whose life has been entirely devoted to spiritual endeavor in monasteries, perhaps allowing for a development of the ministry of others in administering more practical aspects of the Church's life.

Another area where Orthodoxy might choose to return to its roots is in the matter of clergy titles. Calling leaders "Eminence" or "Excellency" is something that rightly belongs to the royal and imperial courts of former times. Mindful of the humility of the Savior, we might do well to review this area of church life in the future, since the glory of the priesthood does not lie in the use of outdated titles.

Leadership within the Church, both from the clergy and the laity, needs to be in a constant state of repentance, ever returning to the incisive and difficult words of Jesus, "And whoever of you desires to be first shall be slave of all" (Mark 10:44).

Postscript

*Y*ou've got to get out of your head and into your heart. Right
now your thoughts are in your head, and God seems to be outside
you. Your prayer and all your spiritual exercises also remain exte-
rior. As long as you are in your head, you will never master your
thoughts, which continue to whirl around your head like snow in
a winter's storm or like mosquitoes in the summer's heat. If you
descend into your heart, you will have no more difficulty. Your mind
will empty out and your thoughts will dissipate. Thoughts are always
in your mind chasing one another about, and you will never manage
to get them under control. But if you enter into your heart and can
remain there, then every time your thoughts invade, you will only
have to descend into your heart and your thoughts will vanish into
thin air. This will be your safe haven. Don't be lazy. Descend. You
will find life in your heart. There you must live.

—ST. THEOPHAN THE RECLUSE[16]

It is worth remembering that it is the act of seeking the place of the
heart which is our goal, our highest aspiration, not the actual finding
of it. It is the journey, not the destination, which is of utmost importance. Of course, some saints may (and do) actually find the destination, but that is (as it were) another story, for another day.

---

16 As quoted in Jean-Yves Leloup, *Being Still: Reflections on an Ancient Mystical
Tradition* (New York: Paulist Press, 2003), p. 124.

About the Author

ARCHIMANDRITE MELETIOS WEBBER IS AN ORTHO-
dox priest. He was received into the Orthodox Church by Bishop
Kallistos Ware in 1971. He was educated at Dulwich College and
Oxford University, and has a doctorate in psychological counseling.
Fr. Meletios has served the Orthodox Church in Greece, Great Brit-
ain, Montana, and California, and is currently living in the Nether-
lands. He is the author of *Steps of Transformation: An Orthodox Priest
Examines the Twelve Steps* (Conciliar Press, 2003).

Other Books of Interest from Conciliar Press

A Beginner's Guide to Prayer
by Fr. Michael Keiser

This is a book for those struggling to establish an effective life of prayer. Written neither for seasoned monastic nor lofty scholar, *A Beginner's Guide to Prayer* speaks to the average man or woman on the street who desires a deeper relationship with God but is unsure how or where to begin. Drawing from nearly 2000 years of Orthodox spiritual wisdom, the author offers warm, practical, pastoral advice whose genius is to be found in its homespun simplicity and straightforwardness of style.

If you've been desiring to make prayer a meaningful and regular part of your life, *A Beginner's Guide to Prayer* will help set you on your way. But be careful—prayer can be habit-forming! In fact, the advice offered in this book may just change the course of your life. So, in the words of the author, "What are you waiting for? Start to pray!" (ISBN 13: 978-1-888212-64-8)

A Beginner's Guide to Spirituality
by Fr. Michael Keiser

Spirituality is in! Monks go platinum with recordings of chant and books on self-help spirituality overflow supermarket bookracks. But what is the meaning of true spirituality? Aren't we all a little confused? Genuine spirituality keeps us in balance with God, our neighbor, and the material world.

Fr. Michael Keiser walks us through the Orthodox Church's timeless teachings and practices on the ancient understanding of Christian spirituality with humor and keen insight. He outlines how ascetic practices, personal and corporate worship, confession and repentance, overcoming the passions, and opening ourselves up to God's grace can lead us to transformation and to our ultimate destiny—Jerusalem, the heavenly city. (ISBN 13: 978-1-888212-88-4)

Let Us Attend! A Journey Through the Orthodox Divine Liturgy
by Fr. Lawrence Farley

Esteemed author and Scripture commentator Fr. Lawrence Farley gives us a guide to understanding the Divine Liturgy, and a vibrant reminder of the centrality of the Eucharist in living the Christian life. Every Sunday morning we are literally taken on a journey into the Kingdom of God. Fr. Lawrence guides believers in a devotional and historical walk through the Orthodox Liturgy. Examining the Liturgy section by section, he provides both historical explanations of how the Liturgy evolved and devotional insights aimed at helping us pray the Liturgy in the way the Fathers intended. In better understanding the depth of the Liturgy's meaning and purpose, we can pray it properly.

If you would like a deeper understanding of your Sunday morning experience so that you can draw closer to God, then this book is for you. (ISBN 13: 978-1-888212-87-7)

Ascending the Heights
by Fr. John Mack

In the sixth century, a monk named John wrote a book outlining the stages of the spiritual life. He based his entire work on the image of a ladder of thirty rungs stretching from earth to heaven. Each rung described a step in the pursuit of virtue and the spiritual life. Since it was first written, *The Ladder of Divine Ascent* has been an essential part of the formation of Orthodox monastics and a mainstay of Orthodox ascetic spirituality. But it is not just for monks and nuns.

This book was written to help those in a non-monastic setting understand how to apply *The Ladder of Divine Ascent* to their lives. Each chapter contains many direct quotes from St. John's writings, in addition to commentary. This book, therefore, should be used as a primer to the *Ladder*—as a helpful tool for ascending the spiritual heights. (ISBN 13: 968-1-888212-17-4)

The Jesus Prayer: A Gift from the Fathers
by Fr. David Hester

"O Lord Jesus Christ, Son of God, have mercy on me." This prayer has been on the lips of Christians since the time of the Desert Fathers. What is its history? How do we make it our own? This booklet traces the development of the Jesus Prayer through the early centuries of the Church and follows its progression through Mount Athos, the teachings of St. Gregory Palamas and others, and discusses its modern revival in the 19th and 20th centuries. Concludes with a brief discussion of how this prayer can be appropriated by the individual believer today. (ISBN 13: 978-1-888212-26-6)

To request a Conciliar Press catalog, to obtain current pricing or ordering information, or to place a credit card order, please call Conciliar Press at (800) 967-7377 or (831) 336-5118, or log onto our website: www.conciliarpress.com